WINDOWS® PHONE 7
Companion

WINDOWS® PHONE 7
Companion

MATTHEW MILLER

Wiley Publishing, Inc.

Windows® Phone 7 Companion
Published by
Wiley Publishing, Inc.
10475 Crosspoint Boulevard
Indianapolis, IN 46256
www.wiley.com
Copyright © 2011 by Wiley Publishing, Inc., Indianapolis, Indiana

Published simultaneously in Canada

ISBN: 978-0-470-93856-0
ISBN: 978-1-118-02537-6 (ebk)
ISBN: 978-1-118-02418-8 (ebk)
ISBN: 978-1-118-02419-5 (ebk)

Manufactured in the United States of America

10 9 8 7 6 5 4 3 2 1

For general information on our other products and services please contact our Customer Care Department within the United States at (877) 762-2974, outside the United States at (317) 572-3993 or fax (317) 572-4002.

Wiley also publishes its books in a variety of electronic formats. Some content that appears in print may not be available in electronic books.

Library of Congress Control Number: 2010939950

My Savior, Jesus Christ, has blessed me with the technical and writing abilities needed to write this book and everything I have I owe to Him.

＋ ABOUT THE AUTHOR

 **MATTHEW (PALMSOLO) MILLER** began using mobile devices in 1997 and has been writing online for Geek.com and then ZDNet since 2001. He is a professional engineer and naval architect in Seattle who served for 12 years in the U.S. Coast Guard after graduating from the USCG Academy in 1993.

Matthew began writing daily news posts and conducting reviews for Geek.com in 2001. He co-authored the *Master Visually 2003* book in 2004. In 2006, he launched The Mobile Gadgeteer technical blog on ZDNet and then expanded to his Smartphone & Cell Phones blog (`blogs.zdnet.com/cell-phones`) as the smartphone market took off and required a site focused just on mobile phones. Matthew also has a passion for Nokia devices and launched the Nokia Experts website (`nokiaexperts.com`) in January 2009. You can follow Matthew on Twitter at `twitter.com/palmsolo`.

Matthew is also a husband to his beautiful wife of more than 17 years, Dayna, and a father to his three daughters, Danika, Maloree, and Kari. He enjoys playing and coaching sports, camping with the family, and catching all the latest movies.

ABOUT THE TECHNICAL EDITOR

TODD MEISTER has been developing and using Microsoft technologies for over fifteen years. He's been a technical editor on over 75 titles ranging from SQL Server to the .NET Framework. Besides doing technical editing, he is the Senior IT Architect at Ball State University in Muncie, Indiana. He lives in central Indiana with his wife, Kimberly, and their four amusing children.

CREDITS

Executive Editor
Carol Long

Senior Project Editor
Adaobi Obi Tulton

Technical Editor
Todd Meister

Senior Production Editor
Debra Banninger

Copy Editor
Apostrophe Editing Services

Editorial Director
Robyn B. Siesky

Editorial Manager
Mary Beth Wakefield

Freelancer Editorial Manager
Rosemarie Graham

Associate Director of Marketing
David Mayhew

Production Manager
Tim Tate

Vice President and Executive Group Publisher
Richard Swadley

Vice President and Executive Publisher
Barry Pruett

Associate Publisher
Jim Minatel

Project Coordinator, Cover
Lynsey Stanford

Compositor
Maureen Forys,
Happenstance Type-O-Rama

Proofreader
Word One

Indexer
Robert Swanson

Cover Image
Wiley In-house Design

Cover Designer
Ryan Sneed

╋ ACKNOWLEDGMENTS

I would like to thank my wife, Dayna, for her patience and understanding with my late nights and deadlines and for helping to keep me motivated to complete this book in record time. I thank my three wonderful daughters for giving me the quiet time I needed and for the hugs when I was feeling down. My good friend and mentor, Joel Evans, gave me my first writing opportunity, and I am blessed to be writing with him again on ZDNet. There were many people at Microsoft and HTC over the years who I had the pleasure of working with and becoming friends with, including Jason Gordon, John Starkweather, Eric Lin, and Jeff McKean. Patrick Neighorn was instrumental in getting me a prototype Windows Phone 7 device to use and in answering questions about the OS that I struggled with, so without his efforts I would not have accepted this exciting project, and I greatly appreciate the help. I thank all my readers at ZDNet who visit my blogs on a regular basis and continue to make daily writing about mobile phones an enjoyable second career. I want to thank Carol Long from Wiley for accepting me as the book author when initial plans didn't work out. My senior project editor at Wiley, Adaobi Obi Tulton, did an amazing job of providing valuable feedback and helping me and her team complete this project on a timely basis to release when Windows Phone 7 devices launched.

+ CONTENTS AT A GLANCE

✛ CONTENTS

INTRODUCTION

If you opened this book with preconceived notions that another mobile operating system from Microsoft could never match the usability and speedy response of the Apple iPhone, throw those thoughts right out of the window. Microsoft completely scrapped its old Pocket PC and Windows Mobile strategy to take the desktop experience to the palm of your hand and started from scratch with Windows Phone 7.

What you are about to experience and learn all about is something completely new and fresh, with a splash of art and modern design. Microsoft threw away scrollbars and instead is using text flowing across the display to let you know that you can discover more. The new user interface is known as Metro and is designed to help you "find your way" across the phone and the information that you are led to.

You may see the terms *pivot* and *panorama* used in Windows Phone 7's user interface; these are the control methods to navigate in the OS. With pivot the developer provides you with a quick way to manage views or pages and is why you see text flowing in headers to the right and left: Tapping partial text moves you right or left. The panorama control is visible when you slide up and down a display vertically; the Start screen reaches down vertically virtually without limit.

You will also discover a consistency across and through the platform that even extends into third-party applications. Microsoft knew that to be successful in the smartphone world today, it had to take back control of its platform to provide consumers with the best experience that is also easily updated as new features are added or improved upon.

Combined with flowing text, fluid touch motions are a focus of Windows Phone 7, so your fingers can slide, flick, pinch, spread, tap, tap and hold, and double-tap. Everything responds nearly instantly and it truly is a breath of fresh air to use and engage with. It is different than anything you have seen before, and just about everyone who has tried out Windows Phone 7 has been impressed.

Media and gaming are enhanced on Windows Phone 7 and bring an experience second to none while still meeting the needs of the prosumer who needs to get his email from various accounts or even view and edit an Office document on the go. Windows Phone 7 is completely new, so this book is designed to serve as your companion and help you discover the power in your hand.

Although the user interface is quick and easy to navigate, there is actually quite a bit of depth in these devices, and with this book we hope to enrich your Windows Phone 7 experience. It is not just for the new Windows Phone 7 user (aren't we all though?), but also for the more advanced users looking for some tips and tricks to using their new device.

I discovered more than I ever thought possible with Windows Phone 7 while writing this book and hope you are as excited as I am about this new mobile operating system from Microsoft.

CHAPTER ONE

HOW DO I SET UP AND CUSTOMIZE MY WINDOWS PHONE 7 DEVICE?

In this chapter:

+ Initial Startup and Login Screens
+ Understanding the Windows Phone 7 Start and Application Launcher Screens
+ What Is the Difference Between a Hub and a Tile?
+ Customizing the Start Screen and Tiles
+ Configuring Basic Phone Settings
+ Setting Up Keyboard Preferences
+ Password Protecting Your Phone

Microsoft has learned from other mobile operating systems over the past few years, and now the setup of your new Windows Phone 7 device is quick and simple. You step through a handy, self-explanatory wizard, and like magic all your email, photos, status updates, and more appear on your device within minutes. Because the user experience is vastly different on Windows Phone 7 than on previous Microsoft mobile operating systems, you need to understand some basic elements out-of-the-box so that you can start using your new device.

Initial Startup and Login Screens

After unboxing your Windows Phone device and connecting the charger to fully charge the battery for use, turn it on using the physical power switch. Carrier logos and startup screens may appear, but then you should see a welcome screen stating, "Let's get started." Let's now walk through the initial startup:

1. At the welcome screen you should see two buttons along the bottom, one to make an emergency call and the other to get started. Don't make an emergency call to get help setting up your device; the emergency call button is for serious emergencies only. Touch on the Get Started button to continue.

2. This next screen shows you the Windows Phone terms of use with hyperlinks to the full Terms of Use and Privacy Statement pages. Read through these if you like, but most of us never do because we pretty much know what to expect with a mobile phone. If you select the Reject option, the phone shuts down. Touch on the Accept button to continue.

3. You now have two options for setting up your Windows Phone (see Figure 1-1); either use the recommended settings or custom settings. These options actually just control the settings to send information to Microsoft to help improve its product (a fairly typical Microsoft setting on its products) and by selecting Custom you can uncheck this box. Touch on Recommended to continue setup.

4. Tap your time zone if it is different than the one predicted through your carrier wireless connection. Tap Next to continue the wizard.

5. This next display is where the magic starts, and you have three options for entering your Windows Live ID (see Figure 1-2). You can sign in to an existing Live account (this includes your Xbox LIVE, Zune, Hotmail, or Messenger account, if you have one), create a new one, or select Not Now. If you choose not to sign in with or create a Windows Live ID, the device has limited functionality, which is not advised. If you purchased a Microsoft Windows Phone device, you already understand that this is a Microsoft product so there is no reason not to sign in and enjoy the full Windows Phone experience. Tap Sign In to sign in to your existing account. If you need to create a new Live ID, tap Create One and follow the couple of steps to complete this account setup.

6. Enter your Windows Live ID (an existing one or one you just created) and password. Tap the Sign In button to continue.

7. The final display states All done. Have fun! Tap the Done button to finish the initial setup process.

After following these few steps to set up and log in to your Windows Phone 7 device, you see the main Start screen while all your Windows Live information continues to sync to your new phone in the background. See Chapter 5 to set

FIGURE 1-1 You have two available options for setting up your Windows Phone.

FIGURE 1-2 Make sure to choose Sign In or Create One for the best Windows Phone experience.

up other accounts and customize the Windows Live default account you set up during the initial startup process.

Understanding the Windows Phone 7 Start and Application Launcher Screens

In the past Microsoft took the Start button and Start bar experience from the desktop to the mobile device, but that association is no longer the driving force behind Start on Windows Phone 7.

After completing the initial setup process, you see the main Start screen of your Windows Phone 7 device with blocks appearing on the display (see Figure 1-3). These blocks, called tiles, appear as either two across or one across the screen with a scrolling vertical design so that tiles can appear down for several screens. The Start and application launcher screens do not support landscape orientation. The number of viewable tiles on one display varies depending on the size of your Windows Phone display, but generally you can see up to four tiles high on one display. We discuss these tiles in more detail in the next sections, but they are all different with some animated and others having different colors and backgrounds.

Pressing the center Start button on your Windows Phone always take you back to the top of this main Start screen, so you eventually want to place your most-used tiles at the top of the Start screen.

You can slide your finger up and down on the Start screen to see all of the items on your Start screen, but if you slide your finger from right to left, you can find the other main display, the application launcher. You can also tap the right-facing arrow in the upper-right corner to go to the application launcher screen (see Figure 1-4). The application launcher screen simply shows all your applications, six hubs, and email accounts sorted in alphabetical order with small icons to the left and the name of the application/hub/email account on the right. Note that the arrow is now in the upper left and points to the left.

END OF THE ROAD ANIMATION Did you notice the animation that happens when you reach the bottom or top of the lists on the Start and application launcher screens? The icons compress slightly to let you clearly know you have reached the top or bottom of the screen.

FIGURE 1-3 Note the single and double wide tiles on the Start screen.

FIGURE 1-4 The application launcher screen shows all your apps and accounts in alphabetical order.

You cannot sort these in a different manner, organize them with folders and subfolders, or remove them from the list. The only option available to you is access by tapping and holding on one of the items to pin to Start so that you can have access to it from the main Start screen.

What Is the Difference Between a Hub and a Tile?

Let's go back and look closer at the Start screen of your Windows Phone 7 device. You can notice that the Start screen is populated by several tiles by default that include tiles for utilities, apps, accounts, and hubs. You can also add tiles for specific people, Internet favorites, and more that the next section, "Customizing the Start Screen and Tiles," discusses. Hubs appear as tiles on the Start screen but are central focal points for your Windows Phone and are doorways into a broader mix of content related to each other through the Internet, services, and applications.

The six hubs in Windows Phone 7 can all be pinned to the Start screen. Following are the hub descriptions as stated in Microsoft's press release:

+ **People**: Delivers an engaging social experience by bringing together relevant content based on people, including their live feeds from social networks and photos. It also provides a central place to post updates to Facebook and Windows Live in one step.

+ **Pictures**: Makes it easy to share pictures and video with a social network in one step. Windows Phone 7 also brings together a user's photos by integrating with the Web and PC, making the phone the ideal place to view a person's entire picture and video collection.

+ **Games**: Delivers the first and only official Xbox LIVE experience on a phone, including Xbox LIVE games, Spotlight feed, and the capability to see a gamer's avatar, achievements, and gamer profile. With more than 23 million active members around the world, Xbox LIVE unlocks a world of friends, games, and entertainment on Xbox 360 and now also on Windows Phone 7.

+ **Music and Video**: Creates an incredible media experience that brings the best of Zune, including content from a user's PC, online music services, and even a built-in FM radio into one simple place that is all about music and video. Users can turn their media experience into a social one with Zune Social on a PC and share their media recommendations with like-minded music lovers. The playback experience is rich and easy to navigate and immerses the listener in the content.

+ **Marketplace**: Enables the user to easily discover and load the phone with certified applications, games, and music.

+ **Office**: Brings the familiar experience of the world's leading productivity software to the Windows Phone. With access to Office, OneNote, and SharePoint Workspace all in one place, users can easily read, edit, and share documents. With the additional power of Outlook Mobile, users stay productive and up to date while on the go.

Tapping one of these hubs takes you to the launch screen for that hub where you have access to services, apps, and content associated with that hub.

If you tap an application tile, such as Internet Explorer Mobile, that specific application launches. You can create tiles for specific people, which are detailed in Chapter 4. Tiles are also generated when you set up an email account so that you have account tiles that give you direct access to the email account. A phone tile is created and appears in the upper-left corner by default, so you can quickly make phone calls on your new smartphone.

Some tiles dynamically change without any action on your part; These are known as Live Tiles. The People tile changes the faces of people as status updates appear; the calendar tile changes dates and appointments as time goes on; your email tiles pop up numbers as unread emails stack up in your inbox; and your Games tile has an active Xbox LIVE avatar entertaining you as you look at your start screen.

Customizing the Start Screen and Tiles

Now that you understand a bit more about what appears on your Start screen, you may be wondering if you can change any of it. Double-wide and single-wide tiles appear here. This width is controlled by Microsoft and application developers, so you cannot change a tile's width; there are even limitations on third-party apps with double-wide tiles. Double-wide tiles are loaded be default for Pictures and Calendar information whereas single-wide tiles are the primary tile design form factor.

You can add and remove apps, contacts, utilities, accounts, and more to the Start screen, you can rearrange tiles, and you can change your theme, so let's take a closer look at each of these functions.

ADDING AND REMOVING TILES

Tiles that appear on the Start screen are pinned to the Start menu. You can remove tiles and pin objects to the Start menu by simply tapping and holding on objects and selecting Pin to Start (see Figure 1-5) or tapping the Pushpin icon with the slash through it in the upper-right corner, see Figure 1-6.

FIGURE 1-5 Note the pop-up that appears when you tap and hold on an icon.

REARRANGING TILES

Unlike the alphabetical order of your application launcher screen, you do have some limited
control over your Start menu tiles. To rearrange
tiles, follow these steps:

1. Tap and hold on a tile. You see it pop
   to the front while the rest of the Start
   screen fades a bit into the back. A
   Pushpin icon with a slash through it
   appears in the upper-right corner.

2. To place the tile in a different location, simply hold your finger on the tile and move
   it around the display. Other tiles move to
   make room as you move the tile around so
   that you can see how it can fit in.

3. Tap outside the tile area (right or left) and
   the tile moving function turns off and
   takes you back to your Start screen.

FIGURE 1-6 You can tap
the crossed Pushpin icon to
remove Xbox LIVE from the
Start screen.

TILTING PLACEMENT INDICATORS As you drag a tile around the display, the tiles underneath "tilt" up or down. If tiles tilt toward the top, your
moved tile appear above the tile you are hovering over; if tiles tilt down,
your moved tile will be placed on the row below the tile.

As you move tiles around, you might have empty spaces adjacent to the
single-width tiles, so spend some time fitting everything together so to optimize your space.

CHOOSING A THEME

You cannot add a custom background image behind the tiles or customize
many other aspects of your Windows Phone, which is a bit different than what
we have seen on Windows Mobile in the past. However, you can change the

theme, which then changes fonts throughout the platform, tile colors, signal indicator balls, and more to give you a consistent theme on the device.

To change your theme, follow these steps:

1. Slide over to the application launcher page and scroll down to settings.

2. Tap Settings.

3. Tap Theme. You see options to change the background and accent color, as shown in Figure 1-7.

4. Tap Background and choose either Dark or Light. Dark make the background black whereas Light makes it white.

5. Tap the box below Accent Color; then tap a color you want to use for your theme (see Figure 1-8).

The available colors for your themes change depending on the carrier and device manufacturer. Microsoft specifies that a few select basic colors must be present, but it enables carriers and manufacturers to add more colors for customers to choose from.

FIGURE 1-7 Select from one of two background choices.

FIGURE 1-8 Pick your favorite color for tile and accent coloring.

Configuring Basic Phone Settings

Settings are sprinkled throughout your Windows Phone, you might want to customize a few basic ones as you start using your phone. These settings include turning the ringer on or off, setting display brightness, and setting up your Region and Language settings.

ADJUSTING THE RINGER

Some devices have physical ring/silent switches, but on Windows Phone you simply use the volume buttons to control the ringer. It might not be as simple as a physical switch, but after you learn the process, it is quick and easy.

To adjust the ringer, simply follow these steps:

1. Turn on the display by tapping the Power button. You do not need to unlock your Windows Phone device.

2. Press the volume buttons up or down. A ringer control panel slides down from the top.

3. Tap the Ring icon on the right side to switch to Vibrate mode, or tap the Vibrate icon to switch to Ringer mode.

4. To adjust the ringer volume, simply press repeatedly or hold up or down the Volume button to adjust the volume level of the ringer.

Although this method is the quickest way to toggle between the ringer or vibration, you can also simply press the volume down button and hold it as the left side status goes down through the volume levels and finally ends in Vibration mode.

ADJUSTING THE BRIGHTNESS

Windows Phone 7 devices use various display technologies, including AMOLED (active matrix organic light emitting diode), Super AMOLED, LCD (liquid crystal display), and SLCD (Super LCD). Therefore, you may find the need to adjust the brightness setting for low light conditions or as a means to manage your battery life.

To manage your brightness settings, follow these steps:

1. Turn on and unlock you Windows Phone.

2. Slide over to the application launcher and tap Settings.

3. In the system settings area, tap Brightness.

4. To have Windows Phone automatically adjust the brightness, tap the right toggle switch to turn it on.

5. If you want to manage the brightness, turn the toggle switch to Off and then tap the drop-down box below Level. Select a level you want to use.

6. Press the Start button to go back to the Start screen or back arrow to access other settings.

ADJUSTING REGION AND LANGUAGE SETTINGS

Your device should be set up for the region in which you purchased it, but if you are traveling or want to use different date formats, you have the option to manage these settings manually.

To manage your region and languages settings, follow these steps:

1. Turn on and unlock you Windows Phone.

2. Slide over to the application launcher and tap Settings.

3. In the system settings area, tap Region & Language.

4. Tap Region Format and select a language and country.

5. Tap Short Date and select a desired format.

6. Tap Long Date and select a desired format.

7. Tap First Day of the Week and select a day.

8. Tap System Locale and select a language and country.

9. Tap Browser & Search Language and select a language and country.

10. Press the Start button to go back to the Start screen or back arrow to access other settings.

Setting Up Keyboard Preferences

Your Windows Phone 7 device has an integrated software keyboard designed to provide you with an optimal text entry experience. Some Windows Phone 7 devices also have hardware QWERTY keyboards, but they still have software keyboards that you can use in portrait mode as well.

To manage your keyboard settings, follow these steps:

1. Turn on and unlock you Windows Phone.

2. Slide over to the application launcher, and tap Settings.

3. In the system settings area, tap Keyboard.

4. You have five available options for your keyboard, assuming the English (United States) language is selected. Tap the box in front of the options you want to enable on your keyboard. These options include the following:

   ✦ Capitalize the first letter of a sentence.

   ✦ Suggest text and highlight misspelled words.

   ✦ Correct misspelled words.

   ✦ Insert a period after double-spacing the spacebar.

   ✦ Insert a space after selecting a suggestion.

5. You can then choose to go back to adjust other settings or press the Start button to go back to the Start screen.

Password Protecting Your Phone

Your Windows Phone 7 device carries valuable data, so it is recommended that you password protect your phone in case it is lost or stolen. Microsoft gives you the ability to remotely wipe and even find your phone, but you still want to keep people from accessing your data in the meantime.

It is easy to password protect your Windows Phone; just follow these steps:

1. Turn on and unlock your Windows Phone.

2. Slide over to the application launcher and tap Settings.

3. In the system settings area, tap Lock & Wallpaper.

4. Tap the lower-right toggle bar to enable password protection.

5. Enter a four-digit password twice in the provided boxes.

6. Tap the Done button to save the password.

REMEMBER YOUR PASSWORD If you forget your password and enter it wrong five times, you need to wait at least one minute to try entering it again. If you mess it up again, the wait time extends to two minutes; then another mistake sends it to four minutes, then eight minutes, and so on. A hard reset may be the only way to wipe the device and start over, so do not forget your password.

The next time your Windows Phone goes into Lock mode, you can see that you have to slide up the lock screen and enter your password to use your phone (see Figure 1-9). You also need to enter the password to disable the password lock feature on your Windows Phone, so don't forget your password.

Related Questions

- Can I adjust specific settings for my Windows Live account? **PAGE 57**

- Where can I find out more about Xbox LIVE gaming? **PAGE 165**

- Where can I find out more about getting Zune music on my Windows Phone? **PAGE 69**

- Are there any other settings for my Windows Phone? **PAGE 229**

FIGURE 1-9 Enter your password to unlock and use your Windows Phone.

CHAPTER TWO

HOW DO I GET AROUND MY NEW WINDOWS PHONE?

In this chapter:

+ Details on the Lock Screen
+ Touch Control
+ Top Status Bar
+ Bottom Menu Area
+ Changing Display Orientation
+ Voice Command

The new Windows Phone 7 operating system includes some control and design elements from past Microsoft mobile operating systems but has greatly optimized the experience for touch. You can find valuable information on the Lock screen so that in many cases you never have to turn on the device to get what you need. Microsoft has also enhanced the viewing area of the display so that information is shown only when you want it to appear without large top and bottom toolbars taking up a significant portion of the display. Windows Phone 7 devices are easy to control and offer you a fun-and-fluid user experience unique in the smartphone world.

Details on the Lock Screen

After your device display times out (that is controlled by a setting discussed in Chapter 22) or you tap the Power button to turn off the display, when you press the Power button again, the Lock screen appears, as shown in Figure 2-1. This screen includes several elements: notifications, device status, upcoming appointments, time and date, and a colorful wallpaper image.

- -

SLIDE TO UNLOCK If you tap the Lock screen, the entire screen bounces dynamically up and down. The only way to unlock the device for use is to slide from the bottom to the top.

- -

NOTIFICATIONS

Just because your Windows Phone display is off does not mean that your smartphone is turned off. It still works when the screen is dark; it is just help-ing you save battery life. Thus, email, text messages, status updates, calls, and other information is still received by your device. You can quickly see this information by glancing at the Lock screen.

After pressing the Power button once, you see the display turn on and the Lock screen appear. At the bottom of the Lock screen are dynamic icons that appear only if there is information of that type. If nothing has arrived, no noti-fications appear.

The cool thing is that the icons let you know what kind of information has arrived and tell you how many of each type is waiting for your action. For example, a small Phone icon indicates a missed call, a small Conversation box indicates a text message, and a small Envelope indicates a missed email. The bottom notifications are dynamic icons that help you to make a decision on whether you need to unlock and view the details of the information.

SLIDE TO ACCESS YOUR NOTIFICATIONS Although the bottom icons show you the number of items that have arrived of a specific type, you cannot tap that specific icon and jump right into the application to view the new items. You must slide your finger up to unlock the device and then tap the tile that contains that incoming information.

If you have your Windows Phone in your hand or nearby when a message or call comes in, you can also see some dynamic action occurring on your Lock screen for a short amount of time. Incoming text messages and email appear at the top of the display above the device status information; if you slide up the display as the notification comes in, you go immediately into the message to view it.

Incoming phone calls have a different user interface while the phone is locked, which is explained in detail in Chapter 3.

STATUS OF THE DEVICE

If you look at the top of the Lock screen, you see various icons that are all related to the status of the device. These are also dynamic indicators

FIGURE 2-1 The Lock Screen provides you with your device status, notifications, and more.

that change as the status changes. The type of information found in the status area includes the following:

- Cellular wireless carrier connection strength (bars of coverage)
- Wi-Fi (802.11 b/g/n) radio connectivity and strength
- Roaming indicator (if you are off the standard network)
- Vibration (silent) mode enabled

✦ Battery life indicator

✦ Bluetooth connectivity status

LOCK IS LIMITED Did you notice that the Lock screen does not auto-rotate into landscape orientation when you turn the device? The Lock screen appears only in portrait orientation.

TIME, DATE, AND CALENDAR

Most of the bottom half of the Lock screen displays the time, day of the week, date, and next appointment on your calendar. This area of the Lock screen is designed to present you with quick, glanceable information so that you can tap the Lock/Power button to see what is coming up next on your schedule. None of this information is customizable, and it appears by default.

CHANGING YOUR LOCK SCREEN BACKGROUND IMAGE

One part of Windows Phone where you can customize the device to your personal tastes is in the Lock screen background image, as shown in Figure 2-2. Because you see the Lock screen quite a bit throughout the day, you want to find something pleasing to your eye and also something that quickly tells you if you have your Windows Phone in hand or if you picked up a buddy's phone.

One way to change the wallpaper is as follows:

1. Unlock your Windows Phone.

2. Tap the arrow or slide your finger from right to left to get to the application launcher screen.

3. Scroll down to Settings and tap on the word.

4. Scroll down to Lock & Wallpaper and tap on it.

5. Tap on Change Wallpaper.

6. Select an image from your library.

7. Move your finger around to crop the image.

8. Tap the check icon.

You can load images onto your Windows Phone in various ways, which are discussed in Chapters 7 and 8. Assuming that you have images already loaded on your device (several are provided out-of-the-box) you can also use the following steps to choose what you want for your Lock screen wallpaper:

1. Unlock your Windows Phone.

2. Tap and open the Pictures hub.

3. Find an image that has been saved to your Windows Phone.

4. Tap and open up the image for viewing.

5. Tap and hold on the image. (A menu pops up below the image.)

6. Choose Use as Wallpaper from the bottom of the menu.

7. Move your finger around the screen to crop the image to fit your Lock screen.

8. When you are happy with it (see the bright area outlining the Lock screen) tap the check mark icon (signifies the crop function).

Your wallpaper has now been updated, and you can check out your new wallpaper image.

As you can also see on the Lock & Wallpaper settings screen, you have the option to set up a password on the device to make it a bit more secure, as shown in Figure 2-3. To add a password to the Lock screen, perform the following:

1. Unlock your Windows Phone.

2. Tap the arrow in the upper right of the Start screen or slide your finger from right to left to get to the application launcher screen.

FIGURE 2-2 The Lock & Wallpaper settings allow you to customize your Lock screen.

FIGURE 2-3 Use this settings page to enable a four-digit password

3. Slide down to Settings and tap it.

4. Tap Lock & Wallpaper.

5. Tap the slider toggle to enable a password. The word Off will change to On after you tap the slider bar.

6. Enter and then confirm your four-digit password.

7. Tap Done and your password is set.

Keep in mind you also need to enter your password to disable this setting or change your password, so don't forget it.

Touch Control

Microsoft was the first to launch a color touch screen mobile computer in 2000 that was quite a revolution at that time. From 2000 to early 2010, these devices had resistive touch screen displays that required you to use a stylus, fingernail, or other accessory with a pointed end to navigate the device. Windows Phone 7 brings capacitive touch to the entire platform so that you tap the display with your finger tip, and the electrical properties of the human body activate the display. This enables you to touch lightly on the display and quickly navigate around with a more natural movement of your finger.

Moving around a Windows Phone device is an incredibly fluid experience where you simply swipe your finger up, down, right, and left to navigate the displays. When you find something you want to activate or select, you simply tap it and watch the application open up for your use.

SPEEDY SLIDING Did you notice what happens when you move your finger faster up and down long lists? Yes, the speed of scrolling increases. When you get to the top or bottom of a page, you see the display dynamically bounce, too, giving you an indication you have reached the extreme top or bottom of the particular list of items.

You can also tap and hold, sometimes called touch and hold, throughout the device to enable other actions, such as the ability to save or upload photos, change your wallpaper (as previously detailed), move tiles on the Start screen, select to edit a calendar entry, delete items, and much more. Have fun discovering all of these tap-and-hold functions sprinkled throughout your Windows Phone.

Zooming in and out is also a control function that you model by pinching and stretching with two fingers on the display.

IS THERE A TASK SWITCHER? There is no task switcher on Windows Phone 7. To switch between running applications you simply tap the back hardware button. You can also use Voice Command to launch applications or jump back to the Start screen and tap on the application you want to use.

Top Status Bar

Microsoft wants to help you maximize the viewable area of your Windows Phone 7 device, so it created an experience where minimal information is shown at the top; this information dynamically changes with the application and function you currently use. As an almost universal minimum, you should see the time in the upper-right corner of the display. Other data appears dynamically, depending on the application. For example, when you access the phone functionality, you see the signal strength of your connection appear in the upper-left corner because this is the type of data you need to perform this function.

WATCH OUT FOR INCOMING NOTIFICATIONS If you are actively using your Windows Phone and an email or text message comes in, you see an active notification flow across your display over the top status bar with some data to let you know more about the incoming message. You can tap it before it disappears to view the incoming message.

You can see several more pieces of information on the top status bar, but you have to manually "grab" this bar and "pull it down" to reveal the information. Simply take your finger above the display, and slide it down toward the center of the display to reveal the status information for items such as the following:

* Wireless carrier reception strength (bars)

- Wireless carrier data connection status E, H
- Bluetooth and Wi-Fi connection status
- Vibrate profile enabled
- Battery status

After you slide your finger down to reveal this information, it appears for about 10 seconds. Windows Phone then auto-hides the status bar, except for the time.

WHAT'S UP WITH THE FLOWING DOTS? When you perform actions that require the device to make an active connection (such as surf the Web or send an email) you see five dots, matched to your selected color, flow from the left to the center, pause, and then flow to the right as data is sent to and from the device.

Bottom Menu Area

Windows Phone has many improvements compared to Microsoft's previous mobile operating systems, and having a simple and consistent menu system across the platform is definitely one of the bright spots. If you used an older Pocket PC or Windows Mobile device, you know that various forms of menus could be found throughout the operating system and various applications. Microsoft has now created a consistent experience where menu items appear at the bottom of the display in a minimal default view so that you just see a few select icons at the bottom of most applications, as shown in Figure 2-4.

From zero (some screens have no need for any menu options) to four of these circle icons might appear in the bottom menu area. These icons are dynamic and have various characters

FIGURE 2-4 One to four icons will appear along the bottom menu area.

in them designed to let you quickly know the icon's function. Icons such as Internet Explorer tabs have numbers on them that change as more tabs are opened, so these icons are also used as status icons for some information.

If you are not sure what an icon's symbol means, simply tap the More icon at the far right to see the bottom menu area slide up to reveal the icon name or function and the remaining menu items. Tapping this More icon may slide the area up one level to just reveal the names of the icons or just past half the way up the display to reveal a number of menu items for you to choose. To close this expanded bottom menu area, tap the More icon again, or slide your finger down from the top of the expanded menu area to the bottom of the display.

The bottom menu area changes between every application, so look around a bit and discover what functions are available to you on your Windows Phone device.

Changing Display Orientation

Some applications may offer you a better experience in landscape orientation, but most of the time you use portrait orientation. You cannot turn auto-rotation on or off; support for rotation is provided by the particular application. The Start and application shortcut displays are in portrait orientation and rotating your device around won't switch you into landscape orientation. Some applications, such as email, Internet Explorer (see Figure 2-5), Excel Mobile, and text messaging may be better for you in landscape because you do get a wider display and larger QWERTY keyboard to enter text. Some Windows Phone devices also have physical, slide-out QWERTY keyboards, and when the keyboard is revealed, selected programs automatically switch into landscape orientation because it assumes this is what you want with the keyboard open.

To continue the consistent user experience of Windows Phone, Microsoft has done something slick with the top status bar and bottom menu area so that the icons and information simply rotate 90 degrees to the orientation you move to. If you rotate your Windows Phone to the left, you see the bottom menu area now on the right with the More icon on the top right, while the top status bar will be on the left with the time in the upper-left corner.

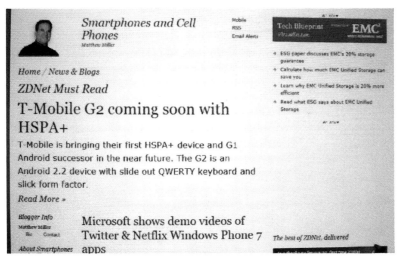

FIGURE 2-5 You can use the Internet Explorer browser in landscape orientation that matches your desktop experience.

RIGHT- AND LEFT-HANDED PEOPLE ARE WELCOME HERE In the past we have often seen that landscape orientation is supported only for rotating 90 degrees to one side, but that is not the case with Windows Phone. You can rotate left or right 90 degrees to enable landscape orientation and optimize the experience for your personal preference.

By rotating your device around, you see only a single-supported portrait orientation; I think this has to do with the physical buttons on the Windows Phone giving you the best experience for control of your device. You may also find that some applications have slightly different methods of handling orientation, and some, such as some games, will not enable you to change orientation. As described in Chapter 13, rotating your device to landscape in Internet Explorer Mobile automatically pops you into full-screen mode with no available menu items or controls on the display. Discover what you can do with your device by flipping it around.

Voice Command

Did you know that your Windows Phone 7 device has advanced voice recognition software that allows you to place calls, conduct searches, and launch applications? Simply press and hold the center Start button on your device to launch the Voice Command software and then speak in your natural voice to control your smartphone. Voice Command is powered by Tellme technology. Calling with your voice is discussed in Chapter 3 and searching with your voice is covered in Chapter 11.

To launch applications with your voice, follow these simple steps:

1. Press and hold the Start button until a pop-up appears on the display.

2. Say, "Start *[application name]*." The software will then repeat what it understands you said or intended to say and then launch the software you stated.

3. There is a cancel button that appears in the pop-up when the voice confirms your statement; if the voice states the wrong software, tap on the Cancel button before the software launches.

So while there is no button for a quick task manager in Windows Phone 7, you can use the Voice Command functionality to quickly switch to another application from within an active application.

Related Questions

+ How do I answer the phone while performing other functions? **PAGE 27**

+ How do I switch my Windows Phone into vibration mode? **PAGE 1**

+ Where can I find games to see if they work in landscape orientation? **PAGE 165**

CHAPTER THREE

HOW CAN I MAKE CALLS AND SEND TEXT MESSAGES?

In this chapter:

+ Making Outgoing Calls
+ Managing Incoming Calls
+ Options Available While on a Call
+ Working with Contacts Within the Phone Utility
+ Using Airplane Mode
+ Working with Voicemail
+ Using Bluetooth with Your Windows Phone
+ Sending and Receiving Text and Media Messages

S martphones today give us the power of a computer in the palm of our hand, but they are still cell phones sold at our local carrier store that enable us to make and receive phone calls and text messages from our colleagues, family, and friends. The great thing is that Microsoft didn't forget this functionality, and Windows Phone 7 devices offer an optimal phone experience designed to make handling calls and text messages quick, easy, and efficient.

Making Outgoing Calls

You always have the option to simply dial a number on a typical touch screen keypad, but Microsoft studied the way people make calls and presents more convenient ways to make calls from your Windows Phone. One of the first things you notice on your Windows Phone that may appear a bit strange is that there are no green (send) or red (end) buttons on most of these new devices, so accessing and using the device as a phone is all carried out on the touch screen display.

CALLING VIA THE PHONE KEYPAD

To place a call using the traditional Phone keypad, follow these steps:

1. Unlock your Windows Phone.

2. Tap the Phone tile on the Start screen or in the list of application shortcuts.

3. Tap the phone Keypad icon in the center of the bottom toolbar.

4. Tap the numbers to dial the phone number you want to reach (see Figure 3-1).

If you used an older generation Windows Mobile device in the past, you notice that the excellent, smart dialing functionality in those phone keypads is currently missing in Windows Phone 7. You could start spelling the name of a contact using the phone keypad to have your

FIGURE 3-1 Use the standard phone dial keypad to enter a phone number.

contacts auto-filtered so that you could more quickly dial a person using the phone keypad. In the current version of Windows Phone, Microsoft took a step back, and the keypad simply enters the number that you tap. Hopefully we will see an update from Microsoft or the device manufacturer that adds this capability back into Windows Phone.

CARRIER IDENTIFICATION Notice under the Phone icon on the tile that your carrier's name appears. This changes dynamically to match the carrier attached to the SIM card or service of your provider, so if you travel to a foreign country and place a new SIM card (subscriber identity module) in your Windows Phone, this will change. In the U.S., SIM cards are currently used by AT&T and T-Mobile while Verizon and Sprint phones are provisioned directly by the carrier.

CALLING VIA CALL HISTORY

Did you notice that the first display that appeared after you tapped the Phone tile was the Call History? Apparently, Microsoft's research indicated this was the most common phone functionality people use for placing calls, and in my experience of using cell phones throughout the years, this matches my patterns and habits of usage, too. Call History (see Figure 3-2 for a typical screen) is also the easiest way to return a missed call. As you can see on the Call History display, the status of the call (incoming, outgoing, or missed) is shown under the name/number of the caller. Missed calls are highlighted in a different color so that they stand out and can be more easily identified.

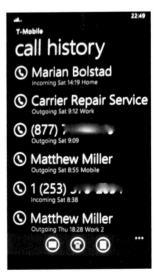

FIGURE 3-2 Your call history is used quite often in Windows Phone 7.

To place a call using the Call History, follow these steps:

1. Unlock your Windows Phone.

2. Tap the Phone tile on the Start screen or in the list of application shortcuts.

3. Tap the Small Telephone icon to the left of the person or number that you want to call.

- -

ACCESSING THE CALLER PROFILE If you tap the person's name or the phone number in your Call History list instead of the small Telephone icon, you see the caller profile. Details of the profile will be covered in Chapter 4.

- -

CALLING VIA THE PEOPLE HUB

If the person you want to call is in your Contact List but is not in your Call History, you can reach them through the People hub. To call one of these people in your contact database, follow these steps:

1. Tap the right People icon from Call History (if you first tapped on the Phone icon from the Start screen) or the People hub from the Start screen.

2. Navigate to the person you want to call, either through the recently viewed page or through your entire list by tapping the appropriate letter (see Figure 3-3) and scrolling up and down in the list, and tap their name. The profile page appears.

FIGURE 3-3 Tap on the letters to find a person.

3. With the person you want selected and the profile open, tap the phone number you want to call.

CALLING VIA START

If you have people that you call regularly, you may also want to consider pinning them to the Start screen, which is similar to the idea of setting up favorites. As you read in Chapter 1, there is virtually no vertical limit to the Start screen, so you can have as many contacts as you want pinned to the Start screen. For contacts you have pinned to Start, follow these steps to place a call:

1. Tap the tile for the person you want to call.

2. Tap the phone number you want to call from the profile display.

INTERNATIONAL CALLING ASSISTANCE To place an international call, you need to start by entering a + in the dialer. To do this you simply tap and hold the 0 key. You can also toggle on or off the international assist feature from the Call Settings display.

CALLING VIA VOICE

Microsoft provides a very powerful alternative to dialing with a traditional keypad or via a Favorite tile thanks in large part to the technology provided by Tellme. With Windows Phone 7 you have an extremely capable voice dialing solution that is as simple as pressing and holding the Start button on your smartphone. As you will see in Chapter 21 you can even set up voice dialing to work with the lock screen enabled.

To place a call with your voice you have a couple of options after you launch the voice dialing speech software. Follow these steps to place a call:

1. Press and hold the Start button.

2. Either say, "Call [person's name]" or "Dial [phone number digits]."

3. The software will then confirm what you said, and if there are multiple numbers for the person, it will ask you which number you wish to call.

4. Confirm the number or name you wish to call by speaking clearly and the software will initiate the call.

The voice dialing software does not require you to train the software for your voice or for the contacts in your database, and it is intelligent enough to provide recognition on the fly.

MAKING A CONFERENCE CALL

Sometimes we need to get more than one person on the phone at once to talk about an issue, and Windows Phone supports conference calling with two or more people. The process is repeated for each caller you want to add to the call; you even have the opportunity to make a selected caller private so that you can talk to them outside of the conference call. To make a conference call with multiple people, follow these steps:

1. Establish a call with one person to start, using one of the methods described earlier.

2. While on that call, tap the down arrow on the right side of the outgoing Call Control panel.

3. Tap the Add Call icon/tile in the lower-left corner, as shown in Figure 3-4.

4. Place a second call using one of the methods described earlier.

5. When the second call has been connected, tap the Merge Calls icon (upper-right corner).

6. To add another caller to the conference call, tap the Add Call icon and place the third call.

7. When that third call is connected, tap the Merge Calls icon to add this caller to the conversation.

FIGURE 3-4 It is easy to make a conference call.

8. Continue to repeat until everyone you want on the call has been added.

While setting up this conference call, you may have noticed that a Private icon appeared as well, as shown in Figure 3-5. You can toggle through the callers, and if you select Private, that caller will be taken out of the conference call and chosen for a private one-to-one call from you that you can still manage and even merge back into the conference call. You also notice that the standard speaker, mute, and hold functions are still present during a conference call. Conference calling is actually a slick experience on Windows Phone, and you can see that making phone calls was not an afterthought on this new mobile platform.

FIGURE 3-5 There are several in-call options while you are on a conference call.

MANAGING YOUR CALLER ID SETTINGS

Sometimes when you use your phone to place calls, you may want to keep your identity hidden from the recipient of your call. To manage your caller ID, follow these steps:

1. Slide your finger down the application shortcut screen, and tap Settings.

2. Slide your finger from right to left to get to the Applications Settings screen.

3. Flick your finger up, and tap Phone.

4. Tap the box below Show My Caller ID To, and select from Everyone, No One, or My Contacts.

5. Tap the Start button, and go back to the Start display to continue using your device.

Managing Incoming Calls

People can also call you on your Windows Phone, so you should be familiar with how to answer these calls. You also need to know how to manage multiple incoming calls, set the phone profile to silent or ringing, send an incoming call to voicemail, and forward calls to another number.

ANSWERING AN INCOMING CALL

Calls can come in when your display is off and the device is locked or when you are actively using your Windows Phone device. You need to take one additional step when your phone display is off. To answer a phone call when your display is off, follow these steps:

1. Notice the Caller Control Panel that appears on your phone display when an incoming call arrives.

2. Slide your finger up the display to unlock the Caller Control Panel, as instructed to by the bar shown in Figure 3-6.

3. Tap Answer to answer the call.

FIGURE 3-6 Incoming call notifications are presented to you on a Caller Control Panel.

If you are actively using your Windows Phone 7 device, the preceding step to slide your finger up the display is not needed, and you simply tap the Answer button on the Caller Control Panel (see Figure 3-7).

You can also receive an incoming call while you are already on a call; if this happens, you have three options on the Caller Control Panel instead of just two. You can choose to answer, ignore, or end the current call and answer the incoming call. If you select to answer the incoming call, your existing call is placed on hold. You then see a control bar, colored to match the theme of your Windows Phone, appear at the top providing you with instructions that state you can tap the control bar to swap between calls. You can then manage each

FIGURE 3-7 Simply tap the button to answer the call.

call individually or even decide to merge the calls and create an incoming conference call.

SETTING THE RINGER

Windows Phone currently has the capability for you to have the ringer enabled or disabled, and the easiest way to manage this is through the use of the volume buttons. Here is how you toggle between an audible ringer and vibration mode:

1. Turn on your device display.

2. Press the volume buttons up or down, and notice the upper volume control bar that pops down from the top.

3. Tap the icon on the far right of this bar to toggle between ring and vibrate modes.

If you decide to turn the ringer on, you can use the volume buttons to set the incoming ringtone volume on your device.

SENDING AN INCOMING CALL TO VOICEMAIL

You may receive calls from people you really don't feel like talking with at the time or calls during a movie or event where you can't talk on the phone at that moment. If this happens you have the option on the Caller Control Panel to simply tap Ignore to send the call directly to your voicemail system.

FORWARDING CALLS TO ANOTHER NUMBER

You may find that you need to send all your calls to another number for a period of time, and your Windows Phone 7 device makes this a quick-and-easy process. I have two mobile phone lines and often forward calls on one account to the other if I will be traveling with just a single phone. To forward calls to another number, follow these steps:

1. Tap the Phone tile.

2. Tap the More icon on the right.

3. Tap Call Settings.

4. Tap the Toggle Switch icon under and to the right of the words Call Forwarding. It should be off by default.

5. Enter the number you want calls forwarded to in the box shown in Figure 3-8.

6. Tap Save to enable the feature.

All your incoming calls automatically go to this new phone number. To turn off this feature, simply follow the preceding first four steps. After you tap the toggle switch, you see it slide from right to left and indicate that call forwarding is now off.

FIGURE 3-8 Enter a number you wish to use for forwarding calls.

Options Available While on a Call

Whether you place the call yourself or receive a call from another person, your main interface for managing the active call takes place on the Call Control Panel that pops up and appears "on top" of the phone display. With this panel you can tap tiles or icons to control the following call services:

+ Speakerphone toggle

+ Mute or unmute the call

+ Place the call on hold

+ Add a call to the current call

+ Merge calls

+ Make call private

You might want to know how to see these available options because you do not see these by default on the Call Control Panel. As you can see, on the Control Panel to the right of the End Call button are the Phone Keypad icon and a Down Arrow icon. Tap the down arrow to see all the available call options, as shown in Figure 3-9; they will dynamically change depending on the status of the call.

CALLS TAKE PRIORITY If you listen to your music or watch a movie during an incoming call and decide to answer the call, your music or movie pauses while you are on the call and then picks up right where it left off when your call ends.

Your Windows Phone 7 device is a powerful mobile computer in your hand, and you can perform multiple functions all at the same time, including using your device during a call. If you have a GSM phone (on a carrier such as AT&T or T-Mobile) you can perform functions using a data connection at the same time as handling calls. For example, you can press the Start button and then check your email, surf the Internet, or use other applications.

FIGURE 3-9 You can manage a second incoming call with a couple of taps.

Working with Contacts Within the Phone Utility

When using your Windows Phone 7 device, you can make and receive calls from numbers not in your contacts database. However, you may decide that you want to add these numbers to your existing database or add them as new contacts to your database for future communication and information sharing. You may also want to assign custom ringtones to specific contacts to make it easier to recognize when people are calling you.

CONVERTING A PHONE NUMBER INTO A CONTACT

Windows Phone makes adding people and new numbers to your contacts from within the phone utility an easy process, as follows:

1. From within the Call History, tap the phone number you want to add to your contacts database.

2. Tap the Disk/Save icon in the middle of the bottom toolbar.

3. Choose an existing contact to add the number to or tap the New Contact option from the display.

4. You can then edit the phone number, if needed, and select the number type (mobile, home, work, company, and so on).

5. Tap the Check/Done icon to save the number.

6. If you add this number as a new contact, you see the new contact creation display (see Figure 3-10) that will be discussed in detail in Chapter 4.

7. If you add this number to an existing contact, simply tap the Disk/Save icon that appears as a final confirmation that you want this number associated with the selected contact.

FIGURE 3-10 You can easily add a number as a contact.

Throughout this process an X/Cancel icon appears in the bottom menu area, so you can change your mind as you work through managing this new phone number.

ASSIGNING RINGTONES TO A CONTACT

Ringtones are a way to customize your mobile phone experience, and Windows Phone gives you the ability to select a preferred ringtone and also assign custom ringtones to specific contacts in your database. To select the default ringtone, follow these steps:

1. Tap Settings from the shortcut application list.

2. Tap Ringtones & Sounds from the main system Settings page.

3. Tap the Ringtone line to select from an available ringtone.

The default ringtone may be acceptable if you don't get a ton of calls, but you can specify a ringtone for each contact in your contacts database so that you won't get confused when someone is calling that you actually need to stand out from the crowd. To assign a ringtone to a specific contact, follow these steps:

1. Tap a contact to view the profile.

2. Tap the Edit icon (with the pencil in the center).

3. Tap the +ringtone item (should be near the top of a list).

4. Select the ringtone you want to assign to the contact.

5. Tap the Save icon at the bottom of the display to make sure this selection was enabled.

Although Windows Phone enables you to select a default ringtone and assign ringtones to individual contacts, you are limited in what ringtone you can select from. Microsoft, manufacturers, and carriers include a default list of ringtones that appear on your device. Currently you cannot select from music on your device or through the desktop Zune client to add custom ringtones to Windows Phone.

Using Airplane Mode

Your Windows Phone 7 device is a powerful mobile computer and media player, so you can use it while traveling on an airplane. You cannot access the wireless carrier network, but you can do many other things with your Windows Phone; increasingly we find that Wi-Fi is provided on flights for connected experiences.

In flight mode you can enjoy Zune music, movies, TV shows and podcasts, play games, work with Office documents, or use a number of other applications. To enable Airplane Mode follow these steps:

1. Tap Settings from the shortcut application list.

2. Tap Airplane Mode from the main system settings page.

3. Tap the toggle bar to turn off your phone's wireless radios.

Enabling Airplane Mode turns off the phone's cellular, Wi-Fi, and Bluetooth radios all at the same time. If your flight supports Wi-Fi, you can enable this radio only by accessing the Wi-Fi settings and tapping the toggle bar.

Working with Voicemail

We can't always accept incoming calls, and sometimes you may choose to ignore the incoming caller. When you tap the Ignore button the phone stops ringing or vibrating and the incoming call goes to your voicemail system. If you do not answer your Windows Phone, the call goes to voicemail by default. You can manage your voicemail number and call into your voicemail system to check any messages that have been left by callers.

To check your voicemail, perform the following steps:

1. Tap the Phone tile.

2. Tap the left Voicemail icon, and a call will be placed to your assigned voicemail number.

3. Follow carrier instructions in the voicemail system to listen to and manage your messages.

Your Windows Phone should have a voicemail message center assigned on the phone by default. If you need to change this message center number, take these steps:

1. Tap the Phone tile.

2. Tap the More icon.

3. Tap Call Settings.

4. Tap the box below the words Voicemail Number.

5. Enter a new voicemail message center number, and tap Save.

Using Bluetooth with Your Phone

Many states have laws requiring the use of hands-free devices to place and accept phone calls while in your vehicle. All Windows Phone 7 devices have integrated Bluetooth wireless radios to enable you to connect to a headset, speaker module, or integrated Bluetooth car systems from your phone. Bluetooth technology has advanced significantly over the last few years, and connecting and using Bluetooth devices is a simple process.

CONNECTING TO A BLUETOOTH HEADSET OR SPEAKERPHONE

The most common use of the Bluetooth wireless connection on Windows Phone is to connect to a headset or speakerphone accessory. Various accessory manufacturers have different passcodes, button presses, and methods for enabling Pairing mode on their headset or speakerphone, but the process to set up your Windows Phone device is fairly standard. To set up your Bluetooth connection, follow these steps:

1. Follow your accessory manufacturer directions, and put your headset or speakerphone into Pairing mode.

2. Tap Settings from the shortcut application list on your Windows Phone.

3. Tap Bluetooth from the main system Settings page.

4. Tap the toggle bar on the right to turn on the Bluetooth radio.

5. You then see a list of devices available to pair with your Windows Phone appear on the display. Tap the name of your headset or speakerphone to initiate pairing.

6. Enter the headset passcode, generally 0000, on your Windows Phone display to complete the pairing process. Some Bluetooth devices will pair automatically without requiring you to enter a passcode.

After you set up a Bluetooth headset or speakerphone for use with your Windows Phone, you can then leave the Bluetooth radio on and manage the connection through the Call Control Panel. To use your Bluetooth headset with an incoming or outgoing call, perform the following steps:

1. With your Bluetooth headset on and the Bluetooth radio enabled on your Windows Phone, initiate or accept a call.

2. Tap the down arrow on the right of the Call Control Panel.

3. Tap Bluetooth Headset to use your headset. You can also toggle off the headset and conduct your call with the phone headset speaker or speakerphone.

You can control various functions from the Bluetooth headset, but this is dependent on the headset manufacturer and the support it provides for Windows Phone. These functions can include the following:

+ Answer a call from the headset

+ End a call from the headset

+ Place the call on hold

+ Mute the call

MANAGING YOUR BLUETOOTH DEVICES

You may end up replacing your Bluetooth headset, adding another headset to your collection, or finding some need to remove a paired Bluetooth device from your Windows Phone. You can add multiple headsets and accessories to your Windows Phone using the pairing method discussed earlier and then the list of devices you have paired will appear on the Bluetooth settings page.

To remove devices from the list, follow these steps:

1. Tap Settings from the shortcut application list on your Windows Phone.

2. Tap Bluetooth from the main system Settings page.

3. Find the headset or accessory you wish to remove from the list.

4. Tap and hold on the name of the headset or accessory.

5. Select Delete from the pop-up display and the device will be removed from the list of paired devices.

If you later find the need to add back that same headset or accessory, you simply follow the steps for pairing and the device will be added back to your list of supported Bluetooth devices.

Sending and Receiving Text and Media Messages

We see more and more people move from making phone calls to sending and receiving text messages because it gives you and the other party a bit more control over when responses are made and in what environment the response comes from. Phone calls are still the best way to communicate where both parties clearly know the tone of conversations and can respond quicker than via text, but it is often more convenient for one or both parties to send and receive text messages. As a father of three daughters, I have embraced text messaging as a primary means of communication on the go because I can send messages out and read ones sent to me when I am not in a meeting, in the middle of a task, or at another time when I have a minute or two to communicate.

WHAT ARE SMS AND MMS? You often see text messaging referred to by its technical name, SMS, which stands for Short Messaging Service. When you send an image via the text messaging service of your carrier, it is called an MMS, or Multimedia Messaging Service, message.

In addition to text messages you may want to share a recent photo that you captured with your Windows Phone; through the text messaging service you can attach photos to your message.

Microsoft provides a friendly user interface for text messaging that centers around the person you communicate with rather than the text messaging application. This matches the overall design of Windows Phone where the experience is focused on the task and not on the application.

There are a couple of ways to hold a text-based conversation with people so let's take a look at them.

INITIATING A TEXT MESSAGE FROM PEOPLE

People are the focal point of a Windows Phone 7 device because you communicate with them on your phone in various ways. You can pin the People hub to your Start screen and also pin individuals you communicate with regularly. To send a text message to a specific individual, follow these steps:

1. Tap the name of the person you want to text with from either the Start screen if you have them pinned there or from the People hub.

2. Tap the words Text Mobile from the person's profile page. A new text message is addressed to this person, and the cursor is placed at the beginning of the text box.

3. Enter text into the text box.

4. Tap the Send icon, which is the left icon in the bottom menu area. The message will be sent, and the operating system will take you to the threaded conversation view in Messaging, as shown in Figure 3-11.

WHO IS TEXTING WHAT? As you text back and forth with a person, a display appears that presents the incoming and outgoing text messages in a view where you can easily follow the conversation. Incoming messages appear on the left, and outgoing messages appear on the right. This is extremely helpful for understanding how best to respond to someone in a conversation. This type of design is sometimes referred to as threaded SMS or conversational SMS.

INITIATING A TEXT MESSAGE FROM MESSAGING

You may also want to send a text message to a new contact or continue an existing conversation, and it is easier to do this from directly within the Messaging application, as shown in Figure 3-12. To send a text message to a phone number that is not in your contact list or have your contact list smart filtered as you spell the person's name in the phone number entry field, perform the following:

1. Tap the Messaging tile.

2. Tap the + (new) icon in the bottom menu area.

3. Enter the phone number or start entering the name of one of your contacts using the QWERTY keyboard.

4. You can also tap the small + icon to the right of the address line to add someone from your existing contact database to the text message.

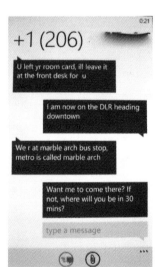

FIGURE 3-11 Threaded conversation view is a great way to understand how to respond in the conversation.

5. Enter a message in the message entry field.

6. Tap the Send icon to send the message.

INCLUDING AN IMAGE IN YOUR TEXT MESSAGE

All Windows Phone 7 devices have a minimum camera specification of 5 megapixels, so you have a fairly powerful camera in your hand. One way to use that camera and share images that you capture is to attach them to a text message; when you do this the message is called an MMS (as defined in the earlier note). As part of the MMS support provided by your wireless carrier, you see that your high-quality image captured with your 5+ megapixel camera is reduced in resolution through the text messaging center. The image is still viewable on the recipient's mobile phone but is not a print-ready photo, as shown in Figure 3-13.

To send an MMS to someone, follow these steps; notice they are almost the same steps as the methods used for sending text messages:

1. Tap the Messaging tile.

2. Tap the + (new) icon in the bottom menu area.

3. Enter the phone number or start entering the name of one of your contacts using the QWERTY keyboard.

4. You can also tap the small + icon to the right of the address line to add someone from your existing contact database to the text message.

FIGURE 3-12 Enter a few lines of text to start a text message.

FIGURE 3-13 You can add an image to your message.

5. Tap the Paper Clip icon (attach) in the bottom menu area.

6. Use your finger and navigation methods to find a picture on your device to attach. You can also tap the Camera icon and capture a new image to attach. You then return to the Messaging application and can see the image you selected appear in the message body.

7. Enter a message in the Message Entry field that is now found underneath the selected photo.

8. Tap the Send icon to send the message.

Related Questions

✛ How do I add people to my contacts database? **PAGE 47**

✛ How do I pin a contact to the Start screen? **PAGE 47**

✛ How do I get Zune media content onto my Windows Phone? **PAGE 69**

✛ Text messages are fine, but how do I send someone an email message? **PAGE 113**

CHAPTER FOUR

HOW DO I CONNECT WITH MY FAMILY AND FRIENDS?

In this chapter:

+ Using the All Screen
+ Interacting with the What's New Screen
+ Viewing and Managing the Recent Screen
+ Adding a New Contact
+ Sort & Display Contacts
+ Importing SIM Contacts

Windows Phone 7 is centered around six hubs, and the People hub might just be the most important one because your Windows Phone is first and foremost a mobile phone. The People hub is optimized for communications with your friends, family, and colleagues in a way to make these communications, including those through Facebook and Windows Live, easy and manageable. You can find three main displays in the People hub with various functionality provided on each.

Using the All Screen

After you set up your new Windows Phone 7 device, you should see the People hub as one of the default tiles on your Start screen. If not, you can always slide your finger from right to left and find People in the list of application shortcuts. People should be pinned to your Start screen because you will use the hub quite a bit to initiate communications with people and to interact with them through Facebook and Windows Live services.

When you first tap the People hub you see the All screen appear by default, as shown Figure 4-1. If you move to one of the other two screens and then pop out of the People hub, then the next time you go the People hub, you can start on the last screen you were on when you left the hub.

WALK AROUND THE ALL SCREEN

The All screen consists of your entire list of contacts from Windows Live, Outlook, Facebook, Google, and other services you have set up with the capability to sync contacts to your Windows Phone. Later in this chapter I show you how to change the order and way your contacts are viewed on the All screen. Let's take a look at the different elements of your All screen and then dive into what you can do with this display.

The top of the display shows the hub name, People. Below this is the name of the particular display we are on, All, followed by a magnifying glass icon in a circle, which is then followed

FIGURE 4-1 The All screen lists everyone in your services databases.

by a circle around a + sign to the right. The circled magnifying glass is a context sensitive search utility that lets you quickly search within your contact database. The circled + is used for creating a new contact; those details will be covered later in the "Add a New Contact" section. Below this is your own profile photo and last reported status update. We are now just below halfway down the first display, and you see the # symbol or first letter with contact names, such as "a" highlighted with your selected theme color.

WHY ARE ALL THE WORDS CUT OFF? Did you notice that the word People is cut off on the right side and bleeds through to the right? This is a common element in Windows Phone that lets you know more information is to the right or left—in this case to the right. If you slide your finger from right to left, you can see the other People hub displays.

You can then simply slide your finger up and down the display to scroll through a long list of all your contacts from top to bottom. You can more easily jump to a particular contact by following these steps:

1. Tap the first highlighted symbol or letter.

2. Tap the letter of the person's name so that you can jump to that section.

3. Scroll up to find the person, and then tap the name. After tapping the name, you see the person's Profile display appear, as we will detail shortly.

USE SEARCH TO FIND FASTER If you have thousands of contacts in your database, tapping a single letter and scrolling through all the names in that letter category may be quite tedious. Simply tap the search icon, and as you start entering text your contact list will be auto-filtered and speed you to the person you are looking for.

You can also tap and hold on a single contact in your list and then select from the following:

+ Pin to Start

+ Edit

+ Delete

Pinning a contact to Start is the way Windows Phone gives you the ability to create Favorites or Speed Dial contacts that you might have seen on other phone platforms.

WALK AROUND THE PROFILE PAGE

After you tap on a particular person in your contact database, you go to the Profile page, as shown in Figure 4-2. By default the first page you see is the contact's profile that shows all of the phone numbers, email addresses, addresses, websites, birthday, and other information entered into the database when the contact was created. Just under the name at the top of the page, you see the names of the services syncing contact data with the selected contact. Windows Phone gives you one-tap access to the following functions from within this profile page:

FIGURE 4-2 You can view detailed contact info on selected profile pages.

+ Initiate a call to a phone number.
+ Start to compose a text message to a contact.
+ Start up an email to a contact.
+ Map the address of the contact in Bing Maps.
+ View the website for your contact.

You can see icons in the bottom menu area that represent the capability to pin the contact, link the contact, and edit the contact. Tapping the right More icon also reveals the Delete Contact option.

The link capability in Windows Phone is a well-designed option to give you control over your contacts because you likely have the contact in various service profiles. For example, many of my friends and family are listed in my Outlook contacts and in my Facebook contacts. Windows Phone gives me the ability to link these together so that I see only a single contact in my People hub, and all the information is available on a single card. Here is how you do this:

1. Acknowledge that the Link icon (small chain) is active (white) and note the number of links shown.

2. Tap the Link icon. A page appears showing you linked profiles already set up, if any, with suggested links below this. You also have the option to choose a contact to link to this other contact if you want.

3. Tap the contact profiles you want to link to this selected contact.

You are not required to link contacts, but this is an option if you notice multiple contact cards for the same person. Windows Phone may suggest linking family members, but that is not required and is entirely optional.

Choosing the Edit option is similar to the new contact creation functionality that will be discussed later in the "Adding a New Contact" section.

At the top and to the right of the word Profile, you can see What's N, and if you slide your finger from the right to the left, you see the full words What's New. This page shows you Facebook and Windows Live status updates for the selected contact. Scrolling down the page all the way to the bottom gives you the ability to tap Get Older Posts if you want to see more status updates for this contact.

A conversation bubble appears to the right of the status update with a + sign or number inside. The number indicates how many comments have been left by others on this status update, and the plus sign indicates no comments have been made yet, but you can tap it to add your own. You can also tap the number to add a comment to the list. Here is how you add a comment:

1. Tap the + icon. It may show a number, which is the number of comments already left, so you can tap the Number icon.

2. Tap in the text box and enter your comment.

3. Tap the right Send Comment icon to post the comment to the status update.

Interacting with the What's New Screen

As you slide your finger from the right to the left after launching the People hub, you find a list similar to the What's New list previously described for a specific contact. Unlike the page in the Contact Profile area, this What's New screen, as shown in Figure 4-3, shows you the latest status updates, from supported services such as Windows Live and Facebook, for everyone in your contact list who has posted an update.

The person's name, the service where the data is coming in from, how long ago the status update was posted, and details of the status update all appear on the left and center of the display. On the right you can find the Conversation Bubble icon with the + sign or number of comments made so far. Note that you can find website URLs, images, and video thumbnails if these were included in the update. Tapping on these opens up Internet Explorer Mobile or the integrated video player on your device.

The What's New screen should automatically refresh when you switch to the screen or when you pop back into it from another application. To manually refresh the What's New screen, simply tap and hold on the words What's New and then tap Refresh.

To add a comment or read existing comments (see Figure 4-4) on status updates appearing on your What's New page, take the following steps:

1. Tap the + icon. It may show a number, which is the number of comments already left, so you can tap the Number icon.

2. View the comments made to the update, and if you want to add a comment, tap the text block that shows Add a Comment in light gray letters.

3. Enter your comment into the text box.

4. Tap the right Send Comment icon to post the comment to the status update.

FIGURE 4-3 The What's New screen shows you the latest feeds from your friends and family.

FIGURE 4-4 You can view and add comments to a person's status update.

WHERE ARE ALL THE UPDATES? You can see a limited number of status updates on the What's New screen, but you can see more if you simply scroll down to the bottom of the list and tap Get Older Posts.

The What's New screen in the People hub shows you status updates from all your synced contacts. If you want to see just the status updates for a particular person, simply tap that person's name in the list of status updates; you go to the personal What's New page with all the latest status updates.

Viewing and Managing the Recent Screen

After launching the People hub, you see three primary screens associated with recent events, as shown in Figure 4-5. Depending on the number of recent communications you have had, you may also find that you have a couple of pages of recent communications that you can access by sliding your finger.

Windows Phone shows you the person's name and latest profile picture from the person's assigned service, such as a Facebook profile photo. The person's name and profile picture dynamically change as you stay on the page.

There isn't much you can do with this screen, but if you tap the person, you go to the Profile and What's New screens. If you tap and hold on a person's picture, options to pin to Start or edit appear. Pin to start will not appear if the contact is already pinned to your Start screen. Edit options are the same as creating a new contact, which the next section covers.

FIGURE 4-5 The recent view shows you your last active communications.

Adding a New Contact

You will make new friends, meet new coworkers, and interact with new clients and others, so you need to know how to add a new contact to your database. You can add new contacts to your new Windows Phone in a couple of ways;

we take a look at these next. The functions described in this section for adding a new contact are the same as for editing an existing contact.

FILLING OUT THE NEW CONTACT FORM

You can capture and enter a large amount of specific contact data into your database, so let's take a look at how to get to these fields:

1. Tap the People hub tile.
2. From the All page, tap the + sign.
3. Enter all the contact details.
4. Tap Save to confirm this data and create your new contact.

Following are a couple of key things to remember as you fill out all the new contact info:

1. Tap the Add Photo box to select from an existing photo or take a photo of the contact manually.
2. Tap the + icon to the left of major field names to expand the fields so that you can enter all the details.
3. Don't forget to tap the Other data label to see the large number of options for adding data to your phone.

You can find the options to designate the phone number as mobile, work, home, company, and fax. The Other data field, as shown Figure 4-6, has options for the following details:

✚ Address
✚ Website
✚ Birthday
✚ Notes
✚ Anniversary
✚ Significant other
✚ Children
✚ Office location
✚ Job title

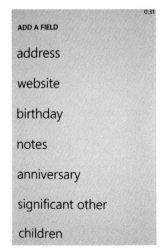

FIGURE 4-6 There are several other fields that you can use to enter detailed contact information.

There may be other custom data fields and you can enter a large number of details for each contact.

ADDING FROM AN INCOMING OR OUTGOING CALL

If you make a call to a new number or receive an incoming call from a number outside your contact list, the number appears in your Call History. With a few quick steps, you can turn that number into a contact that appears in your database.

1. Tap the number you want to add to your database.
2. Tap the Save icon at the bottom center of the display. A contact selector list appears.
3. Tap the + sign in the circle, to the left of the words New Contact. The phone number will be pasted into your phone number line, and another line describing the type of phone number appears.
4. Edit the phone number as needed.
5. Tap the Phone Number Type box, and select which type you want the number assigned to.
6. Tap the Check icon to confirm this new entry.
7. Enter the appropriate contact details, as previously described.

Sort and Display Contacts

By default, your Windows Phone shows your contacts on the All screen by first name with the first name displayed. You may want to sort and display your contacts differently; you have a couple of basic options for controlling this list.

1. If you are on the People hub screen, tap and hold on the top word People. You can also tap Settings, flick to the right (Applications), and tap People.
2. See the Sort List By options, and tap First name or Last name.
3. See the Display Names By options and tap First, Last or Last, First.
4. Go back to the People hub to view your newly sorted and displayed list of contacts.

Importing SIM Contacts

If you are on a GSM carrier, such as T-Mobile and AT&T in the United States, and had a phone before you picked up your new Windows Phone 7 device, you most likely have some contacts stored on your SIM card. It is typical for a SIM card to enable up to 200 to 250 contacts to be stored on it and transferred between devices.

If you have contacts on your SIM card, follow these steps to get them imported into your Contact database and onto your People hub:

1. If you are on the People hub screens, tap and hold on the top word People. You can also tap Settings, flick to the right (Applications), and tap People.

2. Tap the Import SIM Contacts box, and your SIM contacts will be imported.

After you perform an import, the Import SIM Contacts box shows you a date above it for when you performed the last import.

Related Questions

✦ How do I set up services to connect with people? **PAGE 57**

✦ If I tap on a person's website address, what program starts up and how do I use it? **PAGE 151**

✦ What is Bing Maps? **PAGE 141**

✦ How do I make a call from my Windows Phone? **PAGE 27**

CHAPTER FIVE

HOW CAN I SET UP AND SYNC SERVICES TO MY NEW WINDOWS PHONE?

In this chapter:

- ✛ Synchronizing with Windows Live
- ✛ Synchronizing with Outlook Through Exchange
- ✛ Synchronizing with Facebook
- ✛ Synchronizing with Google Services
- ✛ Synchronizing with Yahoo! Services
- ✛ Synchronizing with Other Accounts

The key to a successful smartphone today is the ability to sync to existing services and accounts you have already invested your time and money into prior to purchasing your Windows Phone. Windows Phone 7 devices have the capability to connect and synchronize with a number of services so that you can enter credentials for these in the initial setup phase and have your calendar, contacts, email, photos, and social networking information on your device within minutes of pulling it out of the box.

Synchronizing with Windows Live

Your Windows Phone is a product sporting Microsoft's operating system; therefore, it makes sense that the Windows Live experience is important and offers you the best experience for service integration. You can choose to skip the Windows Live setup and login (either with a new account or an existing account) during the initial setup, but you cannot enable all the functionality and capabilities of your device, so I highly encourage you to set up an account. Accounts are free, and if you buy a Microsoft phone, you are likely to want the best Microsoft experience on your device.

You can set up your Windows Live account during the initial setup; if you choose to skip it at that time, you can also go back into the settings and set up your account. To set up your Windows Phone for Windows Live during the initial setup, simply enter your Windows Live email address and password into the applicable fields. If you do not yet have an account, tap the option to set up a new account and follow the helpful Setup Wizard.

If you skip the setup at launch and want to add a Windows Live account later, follow these steps:

1. Unlock your device.

2. Slide from right to left or tap the upper-right arrow to get to the application launcher page. You may also find a Settings tile on your Start screen; if so, then simply tap the Start tile.

3. Slide down and tap on Settings.

4. On the System screen, tap Email & Accounts (see Figure 5-1).

5. Tap Add an Account (see Figure 5-2).

6. Tap Windows Live.

7. Enter your email address and password (see Figure 5-3).

8. Tap Sign In to connect.

FIGURE 5-1 The main Email & Accounts settings display lists accounts you have configured.

FIGURE 5-2 Select an account type from the list or use the bottom options to add one manually.

FIGURE 5-3 Enter your email address and password to set up your Windows Live account.

Default synchronization settings will then be enabled for your Windows Live account that include syncing of email, contacts, calendar, photos, and feeds. You may want to customize some of these settings, and Windows Phone 7 provides you with this ability, as follows:

1. Unlock your device.

2. Slide from right to left or tap the upper-right arrow to get to the application launcher page. You may also find a Settings tile on your Start screen; if so, then simply tap the Start tile.

3. Slide down and tap on Settings.

4. On the System screen, tap Email & Accounts.

5. Tap your Windows Live account name.

6. Enter a customized name for the account, if you want.

7. Choose when to download new content (as items arrive, 15 minutes, 30 minutes, hourly, or manually).

8. Choose how much email you want to download (last 3 days, last 7 days, last 2 weeks, last month, or anytime).

9. Check the box to toggle email synchronization on or off.

10. Tap to enter your password if it has changed since setup.

11. Tap to enter the server, only if required.

12. Tap to enable/disable logging.

13. Tap Done to complete the settings adjustments.

MANUAL SYNC IS UNDER YOUR CONTROL Did you know you can always force a manual sync of Windows Live? Simply tap and hold on the Windows Live account on the Email & Accounts screen and choose Sync.

After entering your settings, you see that Microsoft automatically creates a tile for the account and pins it to the Start screen. You can choose to unpin this tile from the Start menu if you do not want it there, but it will always appear on the Full Applications and Shortcuts screen.

WINDOWS LIVE IS WELL INTEGRATED After you set up a Windows Live account, you cannot delete or remove it from your device without first performing a complete hard reset and restoring the device back to the factory configuration.

Synchronizing with Outlook Through Exchange

Unlike previous versions of Windows Mobile, Windows Phone 7 does not enable you to connect and sync to Outlook through a desktop connection. Synchronization through Outlook Mobile on the phone occurs through a wireless Exchange ActiveSync process, so you need to have an Exchange Server provided by your company or hosting service to sync your Windows Phone with Outlook.

Windows Live synchronization provides the richest syncing experience, but Microsoft's Outlook synchronization is also top notch. Whether you choose to set up your Outlook sync at launch or later, you may need some specific account information from your IT department. Let's take a look at what a manual setup would look like and if your IT department has optimized its Exchange Server; some of these steps may occur automatically.

1. Unlock your device.
2. Slide from right to left or tap the upper-right arrow to get to the application launcher page. You may also find a Settings tile on your Start screen; if so, then simply tap the Start tile.
3. Slide down and tap on Settings.
4. On the System screen, tap Email & Accounts.
5. Tap Add an Account.
6. Tap Outlook.
7. Enter your email address and password.
8. Tap Sign In to initiate connection.
9. If not automatically enabled by your Exchange provider, enter your user name, domain, and server. You may have to tap Advanced to see the server entry field.
10. Tap Sign In again to complete the setup.

As you saw earlier with Windows Live, default synchronization settings can then be enabled for your Outlook account; these include syncing of email, contacts, and calendar. You may want to customize some of these settings, and Windows Phone provides you with this ability, as follows:

1. Unlock your device.
2. Slide from right to left or tap the upper-right arrow to get to the application launcher page. You may also find a Settings tile on your Start screen; if so, then simply tap the Start tile.
3. Slide down and tap on Settings.
4. On the System screen, tap Email & Accounts.
5. Tap your Outlook account name.
6. Enter a customized name for the account, if you want.

7. Choose when to download new content (as items arrive, 15 minutes, 30 minutes, hourly, or manually).

8. Choose how much email you want to download (last 3 days, last 7 days, last 2 weeks, last month, or anytime).

9. Check the box to toggle email, contacts, or calendar synchronization on or off.

10. Tap to enter your password if it has changed since setup.

11. Tap to enter the server, only if required.

12. Tap the check box if an encrypted (SSL) connection is required.

13. Tap to enable/disable logging.

14. Tap Done to complete settings adjustments.

As you can see, you cannot get synchronization of photos or feeds (aka status updates) through your Outlook account because these are not yet supported through Exchange ActiveSync.

Synchronizing with Facebook

Facebook is now the largest social networking service in the world, and Microsoft has decided to include Facebook integration within Windows Phone as it reaches out to both consumers and enterprise customers. The Facebook integration enables syncing of contacts, photos, and feeds/status updates with your Windows Phone.

If you skip the setup at launch and want to add a Facebook account later, follow these steps:

1. Unlock your device.

2. Slide from right to left or tap the upper-right arrow to get to the application launcher page. You may also find a Settings tile on your Start screen; if so, then simply tap the Start tile.

3. Slide down and tap on Settings.

4. On the System screen, tap Email & Accounts.

5. Tap Add an Account.

6. Tap Facebook.

7. Enter your email address and password.

8. Tap Sign In to connect.

You can have only one Facebook account set up on your Windows Phone, and there are no controls on photos and feeds in the settings. You do have some control over which contacts sync up to and appear in your People hub.

Synchronizing with Google Services

The latest and greatest smartphone platforms now support syncing through Google services so that you can have your phone sync Google email (Gmail), contacts, and calendar data from the Internet. Windows Phone 7 devices perform this synchronization function through Exchange ActiveSync, and you have the exact same settings and control over what syncs with your Windows Phone as you do with Outlook.

If you skip the setup at launch and want to add a Google account later, follow these steps:

1. Unlock your device.

2. Slide from right to left or tap the upper-right arrow to get to the application launcher page. You may also find a Settings tile on your Start screen; if so, then simply tap the Start tile.

3. Slide down and tap on Settings.

4. On the System screen, tap Email & Accounts.

5. Tap Add an Account.

6. Tap Google.

7. Enter your email address and password.

8. Tap Sign In to connect.

Default synchronization settings are then enabled for your Google account and include syncing of email, contacts, and calendar.

- -

MULTIPLE EXCHANGE GOODNESS Did you notice that you can add multiple Google accounts to your Windows Phone with the same control options? Windows Phone 7 supports syncing with multiple Exchange accounts, which Google supports, so you can have all your email and other Google data synced to your phone.

- -

You may want to customize some of these settings, and Windows Phone provides you with this ability, as follows:

1. Unlock your device.

2. Slide from right to left or tap the upper-right arrow to get to the application launcher page. You may also find a Settings tile on your Start screen; if so, then simply tap the Start tile.

3. Slide down and tap on Settings.

4. On the System screen, tap Email & Accounts.

5. Tap your Google account name.

6. Enter a customized name for the account, if you want (see Figure 5-4).

7. Choose when to download new content (as items arrive, 15 minutes, 30 minutes, hourly, or manually).

8. Choose how much email you want to download (last 3 days, last 7 days, last 2 weeks, last month, or anytime).

9. Check the box to toggle email, contacts, and calendar synchronization on or off.

10. Tap to enter your password if it has changed since setup.

11. Tap to enter the server, only if required.

12. Tap the check box if an encrypted (SSL) connection is required.

13. Tap to enable/disable logging.

14. Tap Done to complete settings adjustments.

FIGURE 5-4 There are several available Gmail account settings.

If you have multiple Google accounts to set up, I highly recommend that you name each one something unique so that you don't confuse them later.

Synchronizing with Yahoo! Services

Yahoo! Mail is an extremely popular service, and Microsoft supports synchronizing with this service from your Windows Phone as well. The only data that syncs with this service is email, but that is probably the most used and most important data that Yahoo! users need access to from their mobile phone.

If you skip the setup at launch and want to add a Yahoo! account later, follow these steps:

1. Unlock your device.
2. Slide from right to left or tap the upper-right arrow to get to the application launcher page. You may also find a Settings tile on your Start screen; if so, then simply tap the Start tile.
3. Slide down and tap on Settings.
4. On the System screen, tap Email & Accounts.
5. Tap Add an Account.
6. Tap Yahoo! Mail.
7. Enter your email address and password.
8. Tap Sign In to connect.

You may want to customize some of these settings, and Windows Phone provides you with this ability, as follows:

1. Unlock your device.
2. Slide from right to left or tap the upper-right arrow to get to the application launcher page. You may also find a Settings tile on your Start screen and if so, then simply tap the Start tile.
3. Slide down and tap on Settings.
4. On the System screen, tap Email & Accounts.
5. Tap your Yahoo! Mail account name.
6. Enter a customized name for the account, if you want.

7. Choose when to download new content (every 15 minutes, 30 minutes, hourly, every 2 hours, or manually).

8. Choose how much email you want to download (last 7 days, last 2 weeks, last month, or anytime).

9. Enter your name as you want it shown on email messages.

10. Tap to enter your username, password, and server, only if required.

11. Tap the check box if the outgoing server requires authentication.

12. Tap the check box to use the same user-name and password for sending email.

13. Figure 5-5 shows the advanced settings with options for an outgoing SMTP server address, SSL for incoming email, and SSL for outgoing email.

14. Tap Done to complete settings adjustments.

FIGURE 5-5 You may have to change some of the Yahoo! Mail advanced settings.

Synchronizing with Other Services

Microsoft enables synchronization with key Microsoft services and other popular email and social networking services, but there will still be some people with other POP/IMAP email accounts (such as accounts from a cable or DSL provider) that need to get this information on their Windows Phones. Windows Phone 7 supports other services so that you can have several ser-vices synced to your device and go out and about with all your data.

To add a POP or IMAP email account, follow these steps:

1. Unlock your device.

2. Slide from right to left or tap the upper-right arrow to get to the appli-cation launcher page. You may also find a Settings tile on your Start screen; if so, then simply tap the Start tile.

3. Slide down and tap on Settings.

4. On the System screen, tap Email & Accounts.

5. Tap Add an Account.

6. Tap Other Account.

7. Enter your email address and password.

8. Tap Sign In to connect. Windows Phone 7 attempts to auto-configure the account by searching known ISP data; if its servers find this data, the account can be set up and bounce you back to the Email & Accounts screen.

You may want to customize some of these settings, and Windows Phone provides you with this ability, as follows:

1. Unlock your device.

2. Slide from right to left or tap the upper-right arrow to get to the application launcher page. You may also find a Settings tile on your Start screen; if so, then simply tap the Start tile.

3. Slide down and tap on Settings.

4. On the System screen, tap Email & Accounts.

5. Tap the new account you just set up.

6. Enter a customized name for the account, if you want.

7. Choose when to download new content (every 15 minutes, 30 minutes, hourly, every 2 hours, or manually).

8. Choose how much email you want to download (last 7 days, last 2 weeks, last month, or anytime).

9. Enter your name as you want it shown on email messages.

10. Tap to enter your username, password, and server, only if required.

11. Tap the checkbox if the outgoing server requires authentication.

12. Tap the checkbox to use the same username and password for sending email.

13. There is a box for advanced settings, and tapping this gives you options for an outgoing SMTP server address, SSL for incoming email, and SSL for outgoing email.

14. Tap Done to complete settings adjustments.

Although each of your accounts has specific synchronization settings, you may also want to sync when you are ready; simply tap and hold on an account and choose Sync. You can also see that the tap and hold functionality gives you the chance to delete this account from your device, as shown in Figure 5-6.

Related Questions

✦ Shouldn't I have already entered my Windows Live settings? **PAGE 1**

✦ What can I do with my synced Calendar? **PAGE 123**

✦ Can I upload photos to my Facebook account? **PAGE 97**

FIGURE 5-6 These are the tap and hold options in your account list.

CHAPTER SIX

HOW DO I CONNECT MY WINDOWS PHONE TO MY COMPUTER?

In this chapter:

+ Zune Account Setup
+ Walk Through the Zune PC Software
+ Zune Phone Settings
+ Wireless Sync Capability

I n Chapter 1, I talked about setting up your Windows Phone with multiple accounts, and after completing the Setup Wizard you should see all
your email, contacts, and calendar data appear on your device. In the past,
Microsoft enabled you to use a Windows Mobile device to sync this content
via Outlook and a USB cable. Those days are now gone because all connections to a PC are performed through the Zune software with the major focus
on media content. Contacts, calendar, and email data are synced wirelessly via
an Exchange server, Windows Live, or other service. Actually, if you launch the
Music & Videos hub tile on your Windows Phone, you need to first connect
to a Windows PC to get any media content onto the device, so this chapter
focuses on that physical connection experience.

Zune Account Setup

Similar to the way Apple iOS and iTunes works, you need to take a few steps
to set up your Windows Phone so that it's ready for connectivity to your
Windows PC. You can use your Windows Phone for many functions, including
phone calls, email, text messages, web browsing, and more without connecting to a PC. Let's walk through the steps:

1. From your Windows PC, visit the Zune website at `www.zune.net` and
   click the Free Software Download button; a Zune software download
   page appears. You can also try connecting your Windows Phone device;
   then click the pop-up option Get the Software.

2. Select your version of Windows, divided into 32-bit and 64-bit options,
   and then click on the Download Now button. If you followed the directions in Chapter 1 and already set up your Windows Live account, you
   can also choose Sign Up and Download Now to manage your Zune
   account from a web browser rather than the Zune software.

3. Run the Zune software installation program by double-clicking the
   downloaded file or selecting Run from the pop-up option.

4. Click Accept to accept the Microsoft license terms, after reading them,
   of course.

5. Click the Install button. You can change the folder where the software is
   installed by default by clicking the left Folder icon.

6. A pop-up appears stating that the Zune software installation is complete. Click Close to finish installation.

7. Select the Zune shortcut from the Start menu to launch the Zune software for the first time. The Quickplay screen in the Zune software appears after startup; we discuss this more in section "Walk Through the Zune PC Software."

8. In the upper-right corner, click Sign In, and enter your Live ID credentials (email address and password) to associate your Zune software and Live ID.

CAN YOUR MACHINE HANDLE IT? The Zune software is fairly resource-intensive, so make sure to read the system recommendations section to check your machine. It can run even on an Intel Atom netbook, but you will notice the software takes some time to load and manage your content.

Your Windows PC is now set up with the Zune software; you can explore, discover, and enjoy a huge world. With your Windows PC set up with the Zune software and a Zune account, let's make the initial connection with your new Windows Phone 7 device.

1. Plug the USB cable into your PC and the other end into your Windows Phone. The Zune desktop software should then launch automatically.

2. You see a Windows Phone setup screen appear. This first screen lists what you can expect for the rest of the process including the following:

   + Configuring Zune software

   + Choosing a friendly name for your phone

   + Updating your phone with the latest features

3. Click Next to go to the second step in the setup process.

4. On this screen you can create a custom name for your Windows Phone that shows up in the Zune software when you connect. For the example in this book, I created the device name of WP7 Companion (see Figure 6-1). Click Next to go to the final step.

5. The Zune software will now check the Microsoft servers to see if there is an update for the device (see Figure 6-2). If there is, you can choose to install it now or later. After this, click Done to end the Setup Wizard.

6. You then see the Zune software start with the Phone tab highlighted and your named device on the screen. Setup is now complete, and you can move onto populating your device with media. Details of this are covered in the next chapter.

FIGURE 6-1 Name your Windows Phone as you setup the Zune software.

FIGURE 6-2 The Zune software will check for available updates.

Walk Through the Zune PC Software

The Zune software on your Windows PC is a beautiful piece of software that has a ton of functionality, including a different user interface than most other programs and models. This provides a bit of the same easy flow you experience on your Windows Phone or a Zune HD. There are six main modules in the Zune PC software: Quickplay, Collection, Marketplace, Social, Phone, and Settings. This section looks at some of the key elements of each module, but the software is focused on the user's content, so the best way to become familiar with it is to use it after gaining an understanding of how everything is arranged and designed.

Before diving into each module, let's understand a bit more of the common elements on virtually every screen of the software, as shown in Figure 6-3.

FIGURE 6-3 A typical Zune desktop view shows you several elements for navigation and control.

✦ **Upper left**: A back arrow that enables you to quickly go back to previous screens. Just under this are the main module headings and clicking them takes you to the main display for each of them.

✦ **Upper right**: Links to Settings and Help toward the right corner with your account ID, profile photos, play status, and any available credits to use appear in this corner.

✦ **Lower left**: Your drag-and-drop corner. You should see an icon of your Windows Phone there; to manually get content onto it, simply drag and drop files onto the icon. You can also click your Windows Phone icon to quickly jump to the phone module. There is a CD/DVD icon for creating a burn list to create a CD/DVD of your compatible content. The last icon to the right is used to drag and drop items for creating a playlist or adding to an existing playlist.

✛ **Lower right**: Contains your player controls, so you can control your music experience as you use the software. These controls include Repeat, Shuffle, Back, Play/Pause, Forward, and Volume.

✛ **Center**: The four corners of the Zune software are fairly static whereas everything in the center changes depending on which module you are in, so this center area is where all your discovery and main interaction takes place.

QUICKPLAY

Quickplay is one of the more recent additions to the Zune software and adds some great functionality to the experience. Similar to how you can pin things to your Windows Phone Start screen, you can pin items to Quickplay so that you have faster access to them. Under these flowing areas are sections for Welcome, New, and History with the Smart DJ mix. Clicking an album cover starts the player, and the song plays with animations surrounding the selected album cover. You can see as you move right and left that the displays slide smoothly, and similar to your Windows Phone, parts of words appear on the left and right side to indicate you can slide left or right.

If you click a Smart DJ Mix box below the main area, you see an animated swap occur where Smart DJ Mix is now the primary interface in Quickplay, as shown in Figure 6-4. Smart DJ is a way to launch instant mixes in the Zune software based on any album, artist, or song in your collection and to create automatic playlists for saving and syncing to your Windows Phone. Using the criteria you provide, Smart DJ selects similar songs from your collection and suggest songs from Zune's music catalog.

COLLECTION

The Collection section of the Zune software is where you find everything that you have either downloaded from the Zune Marketplace or imported into the Zune software. Clicking Collection takes you to the main part of this module with the words/section appearing under Collection for music, videos, pictures, podcasts, channels, and apps. Channels are not yet supported on Windows Phone devices but may appear in a future update.

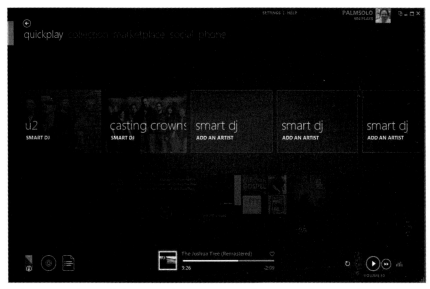

FIGURE 6-4 The Quickplay screen lets you pin your favorites and create a dynamic listening experience.

As you click on each subsection, the album art, movie covers, and so on appear on the left side with details appearing on the right. The placement of content differs with each subsection and sorting option so that the entire experience is rather dynamic. Further filter headings also appear on the right under the Search box that you can use to easily find content. You can also click the headings of each area to view the content in different sorting methods.

In the music subsection, filters appear on the right for Artists, Genres, Albums, Songs, and Playlist. In videos you can find All, TV, Music, Movies, and Other. Hovering your cursor over objects presents you with some options, such as the ability to like or dislike content, so spend some time discovering what functions are available in this area.

MARKETPLACE

The Marketplace is where you go to find and select content for you to enjoy. Subsections of the Marketplace include Picks, Music, Videos, Podcasts, Channels, and Apps. Microsoft looks at your usage patterns and ratings to pick music that attempts to match your tastes, and these predictions appear in the Picks section.

---

10 FREE SONGS A MONTH Don't forget that you get 10 song credits per month with a Zune Pass and can use them to purchase MP3 songs that you can keep and use on other devices forever with no DRM restrictions. Remember though that these credits expire at the end of your billing period and cannot be accumulated so make sure to use them up during the month.

You can choose to download, play, and purchase content from the Marketplace. If you have a Zune Pass, you can download as much content as you want with your Windows Phone with the $14.99 monthly subscription fee. There are various levels of support for subscription services around the world.

As you select artists, you can find several layers of details, including artist bios. The Zune experience is focused on social relationships, and you can check out who else is listening to the selected artist. You can also make "friends" with people who have similar tastes and check out the types of music they listen to because Microsoft tries to create an environment of discovery for the end user.

SOCIAL

The Social section is where you can check out what your friends are listening to with options to add their songs to your collection. At this time, you cannot sync their "card" to your Windows Phone 7 device, but you can see what they are listening to and drag-and-drop it to your Windows Phone. A social card is a customizable status icon that shows people's profile picture, number of times they have played Zune music, and album art of recent songs they listened to. If you click it you can see their recent songs played, favorites, top artists, badges, comments, and profile details. Again, this is a great way to discover new music to enjoy on your Windows Phone.

PHONE

The Phone section of the Zune software appears only after you have made a connection between your PC and Windows Phone. Clicking Phone takes you to the Summary page with available subsections in the Phone module for Summary, Music, Videos, Pictures, Podcasts, and Apps. Clicking each subsection heading takes you to the page showing what content is loaded on your phone. You have the option to delete the content from your phone or add it to your PC collection if you downloaded it directly to your Windows Phone.

Zune Phone Settings

Zune PC software is quite extensive with settings available to optimize the experience for your specific preferences. If you look toward the upper-right portion of the Zune PC software window, you can see the words Settings and Help adjacent to each other. Click Settings to see the following menu options on the left side of the display:

+ Sync Options
+ Sync Groups
+ Name Your Phone
+ Linking
+ Update
+ Wireless Sync
+ Pictures & Video
+ Conversion Settings
+ Reserved Space
+ Error Reporting

Let's now take a closer look at each of these specific areas as you try to customize and optimize your Windows Phone experience.

Sync Options

The Sync Options settings enable you to choose how to sync your music, video, pictures, and podcasts. The choices include All, Items I Choose, or Manual. If you choose All, everything on your PC will sync to your Windows Phone. This option is fine if you have available space on your device storage, but you may want to be a bit more selective with your choices.

If you choose Items I Choose, you need to drag and drop media content from your collection area onto the Windows Phone icon in the bottom-left portion of the Zune software. Any changes you make to items in your collection will be mirrored on your Windows Phone. When you delete something, for instance, it is removed from your phone and from your computer. If you want to keep things on your Windows Phone that you've deleted from your computer, choose Manual Sync.

The Manual choice requires the most interaction from you to get content onto and off of your phone but also gives you the most control.

There is a checkbox to prevent syncing songs you have rated with a broken heart, so you get the best songs on your Windows Phone. Lastly, there are options to Erase All Content and Forget This Phone if you need to disassociate the Windows Phone with this Zune account and want to move to another Windows Phone.

Sync Groups

Music, Videos, Pictures, and Podcasts are the main categories that appear in this area, and when you have Items I Choose selected, sync groups are automatically created each time you drag and drop content onto your Windows Phone. You can also choose to create a group manually with various control options for the source and filters you may want to apply.

Name Your Phone

When you first set up your Windows Phone to work with the Zune desktop software, you had the option to create a custom name for your phone. This setting enables you to go back in and change that name if you want.

Linking

The Linking setting is used by the Zune software for Zune HD players. If you click on this with your Windows Phone 7 device you will see a sentence stating, "Your device isn't compatible with this feature."

Update

Microsoft gives you the option to be informed of updates in various ways, including on the device itself, but this settings area can also give you the specific details of the available updates. You also have the ability to restore to a previous version of the software if you are not satisfied with the updated software.

Wireless Sync

Details on setting this up are discussed in the next section. This area of the settings gives you the ability to set it up or disable the functionality.

Pictures & Videos

Settings here give you the ability to control the import settings, including choosing whether you want to remove or keep pictures and videos on your phone after you sync to your computer (see Figure 6-5). You can also specify where you want pictures imported from your phone saved on your computer. Image quality control can also be selected for syncing pictures from your PC to your Windows Phone with options including the Default for This Device, Original, and VGA (640x480).

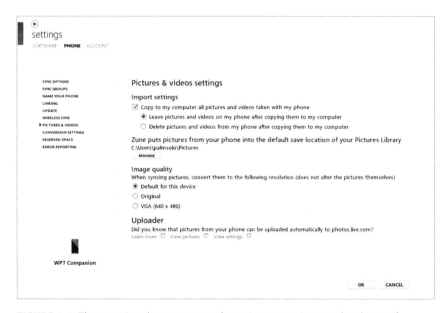

FIGURE 6-5 These settings let you manage how pictures are imported and synced.

You can also enter settings to have pictures you sync from your Windows Phone uploaded directly to `photos.live.com`, so sharing photos with family and friends can be an effortless process.

Conversion Settings

The Zune software is designed to do the heavy lifting for your device so that you can enjoy the content on your device; in the conversion settings you can control the quality of the audio synced up to your Windows Phone. Audio settings enable you to control the bit rate at which songs are synced to your device. You also control the conversion location and the space allocated for conversion in this area of the settings.

Reserved Space

You see a simple slider bar in this settings area where you specify how much space you want reserved on your Windows Phone for things carried out just on your phone and not through a connection with your PC. For example, you need to allocate enough space for email, photos, and videos you capture on your phone; apps you download and install; and more. The remaining space is available for syncing music, video, pictures, and podcasts to your phone from the Zune desktop software.

Error Reporting

This page gives you a single checkbox option if you want to help Microsoft by having error report data sent to them for analysis. Hopefully, you have few errors with your device, but smartphones might experience issues.

Wireless Sync Capability

Many homes have wireless networks that enable people to share their Internet connection with multiple devices throughout the house. The Zune PC software provides you with the ability to sync your Windows Phone device to your PC wirelessly so that you can sync up when you walk in the door without having to connect via a cable.

To set up wireless sync, perform the following steps:

1. Connect your Windows Phone to your PC via the USB cable.
2. Click Settings in the upper-right corner of the Zune software.
3. In the list on the left side, click Wireless Sync.

4. Enable the Wi-Fi radio on your Windows Phone and make sure you connect to your home's wireless network.

5. To the right of the status, click Refresh.

6. After you verify that your Windows Phone is connected to your network, click the Set Up Wireless Sync button. A pop-up for the phone
   setup Wizard appears on top of the Zune software.

7. Verify the network is still correct, and then click Next.

8. Seconds later you should see Wireless Sync Setup Is Complete on the
   display. Click Done to complete the setup.

Your Windows Phone is now set up for wireless syncing, but remember
that a traditional wired connection enables you to also charge your device at
the same time and may be the preferred solution for syncing content to your
smartphone.

After your Windows Phone is connected once with the Zune PC software
then you can download media directly to your Windows Phone without need-
ing to connect to your PC again.

Related Questions

+ How does the Zune Marketplace work with the Windows Phone
  Marketplace? **PAGE 221**

+ How do I check for updates on my Windows Phone directly? **PAGE 229**

+ What do I do if I have a problem with my wireless connection? **PAGE 241**

CHAPTER SEVEN

HOW CAN I ENJOY MUSIC AND VIDEOS ON MY WINDOWS PHONE?

In this chapter:

+ Enjoying Music
+ Watching Videos
+ Experiencing Podcasts on Your Windows Phone
+ Using the FM Radio

M icrosoft included Windows Media Player Mobile on every Pocket PC/ Windows Mobile device, and at first the program was an acceptable choice, given that it closely modeled what was found on the desktop. There was then a period of time where Microsoft had Portable Media Players (PMPs) on the scene, and everyone wanted to see this slick user interface on their Windows Mobile devices. Unfortunately, that never happened, and Microsoft missed an opportunity to roll out powerful media-focused smartphones. PMPs were then followed up by the Microsoft Zune, and since the first Zune was released, people have been asking for Microsoft to bring that media user interface to the phone to create a Zune phone experience. Well folks, that time has now come because your Windows Phone 7 device is a completely functioning Zune phone with support for music, video, podcasts, and FM radio content.

Enjoying Music

The Microsoft Zune HD is the best media player Microsoft has ever produced, and it is a shame that more people do not know about the capabilities and service offerings of the device. Hopefully, including the Zune media functionality on Windows Phone can help educate consumers about the power of the Zune Marketplace and user interface.

To take full advantage of everything Microsoft has to offer, you need a Zune Pass subscription that costs $14.99 in the United States. (Different levels of service are available for different countries.) This subscription gives you the ability to listen to an unlimited amount of music and download and keep 10 MP3 songs each month, so you can build up your own personal library that you can use on any device you want; and if you cancel your Zune Pass, you get to keep these songs. I have been a Zune Pass subscriber for a couple of years and having the ability to try out as much music as I want has allowed me to expand my music listening tastes and try out genres I might not have looked at before if I had to purchase each song or album. Let's take a walk through the process to get your Windows Phone set up and syncing with your music collection.

GETTING MUSIC ONTO YOUR WINDOWS PHONE

As detailed in the previous chapter, every connection between your Windows Phone and your PC is managed by the Zune desktop software. The first thing you need to do is to either import an existing music collection or visit the Zune Marketplace and select songs you want to download to your PC for synchronizing to your Windows Phone. As discussed in the Zune synchronization section in the previous chapter, you can set the music sync to Automatic and have everything you get from the Zune software synced to your Windows Phone by simply connecting your Windows Phone via USB or local network Wi-Fi connection. After you make the connection to your PC via USB, you can also manually manage the music selections placed onto your Windows Phone.

Manually Sync Music to Your Windows Phone

After exploring the Zune PC software, review the previous chapter. To add songs to your collection (via your own personal collection or via Zune Marketplace downloads) follow these few steps to get songs manually synced to your Windows Phone via a USB connection:

1. Connect the Windows Phone USB cable to your device and PC.
2. Verify that your Windows Phone appears in the top row of names (to the right of Quickplay, Collection, Marketplace, and Social).
3. Click Collection.
4. Find songs or albums in your collection, and then click and drag them to your Windows Phone icon in the lower-left portion of the Zune PC software.
5. You can then click the Windows Phone icon and verify that the content has been added to your smartphone.

Purchase and Download Directly from Your Windows Phone

Microsoft also gives you the ability to browse the Zune Marketplace and purchase (even using your 10 monthly Zune credits) and then download songs via a wireless data connection. Following are the typical steps you take to purchase and download songs from your Windows Phone:

1. Tap the Music & Videos hub from the Start screen.
2. Tap Marketplace from the list of items.

FIGURE 7-1 You can quickly view who the top artists are in the Marketplace.

FIGURE 7-2 You can browse the Marketplace by genre.

3. Scroll right and left and up and down with your finger to find songs you want to purchase from the Featured, New Releases, Top Artists (see Figure 7-1), or Genres (see Figure 7-2) screens.

4. Tap the left Play icon on a song or album to hear a preview before you make the purchase. With the Zune Pass you can hear the entire song streamed wirelessly (discussed in more detail in the section "Streaming Music").

5. Tap the song or album name to choose the song or album for purchase.

6. Tap the Buy button to confirm your purchase decision, as shown in Figure 7-3. The song then downloads to your collection.

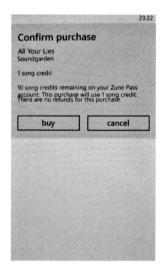

FIGURE 7-3 You can use your song credits to purchase music from the Marketplace.

WHERE CAN I FIND THAT SONG? Search is deeply integrated into Windows Phone 7, so if you know what you are looking for, you can quickly find it by tapping the right Search Hardware button while you are in the Music & Videos hub. Your Windows Phone searches the Zune Marketplace for the search term you enter.

The purchase process is quick and easy from your Windows Phone. When you connect back to your PC, you can have all your purchased music backed up on your PC, too, so you will not have to worry about losing your purchased music if you lose or break your phone in the future.

BROWSING YOUR MUSIC COLLECTION

If you are unfamiliar with the Zune HD experience, I think you will find it extremely enjoyable to browse through your music collection on a Windows Phone device because the user interface is optimized for fluid motions and scrolling effortlessly with your finger on the capacitive touch screen display.

To find songs to play and review your music collection, follow these steps:

FIGURE 7-4 You can choose which part of the Music & Videos hub you wish to visit.

1. Tap the Music & Videos hub from the Start screen.

2. You can now decide to slide right or left to see some of your recently played content; this also includes videos, podcasts, and FM radio, as well as music (see Figure 7-4).

3. Tap Music.

4. Slide your finger right and left to scroll through your music collection by artists, albums, songs, playlists, and genres (see Figure 7-5). If you tap a name of an artist, album, playlist, or genre, you see more information about that particular selection, including other songs by the artist or a quick link to the Marketplace for that artist.

WHO IS THAT ON MY TILE? When you tap artists, the background of the display shows them or album art associated with them. If you then go back to the Start screen, you can see the last background image is now an animated image on your Music & Videos hub tile.

PLAYING MUSIC

To play music on your Windows Phone, simply tap any right-facing arrow (Play icon), as shown in Figure 7-6. This includes tapping the one when you first pop into the Music & Videos hub and see the word Music at the top of the list. By tapping the icon here, you go into a random Shuffle mode that cycles through all your loaded music.

WHAT THIS LITTLE TOOLBAR FOR? There is an cool media player toolbar that drops down from the top. To activate simply tap a Volume button while music is playing in the background to see Back, Play/Pause, and Forward buttons appear for a few seconds. This gives you the ability to control your music while using other applications.

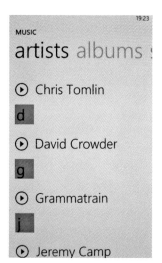

FIGURE 7-5 It is easy to browse through your collection by artist.

FIGURE 7-6 The player controls are found at the bottom of the display.

The key to navigating and playing music is to tap the word for more information and to further dive down into your music library (unless it is a song title); then tap the song title or Play icon to start playing your music.

- -

LISTEN TO MUSIC WHILE YOU SURF Your Windows Phone supports multitasking of some applications, including the music player, so you can have music playing in the background while you perform other tasks such as surfing the Internet, creating emails, or checking out your friends' latest status updates.

- -

STREAMING MUSIC

On other smartphone platforms, streaming music clients such as Pandora, Slacker, and Last.fm have become extremely popular. Windows Phone 7 brings you a similar experience in which you have even more control over the music you stream by integrating streaming functionality directly into the Zune Marketplace.

To stream Zune content wirelessly, simply follow these steps:

1. Tap the Music & Videos hub from the Start screen.

2. Tap the word Marketplace in the list of menu items.

3. Tap the Play icon on a song, album, or playlist, and your Windows Phone connects and starts streaming the content automatically.

CREATING PLAYLISTS

As you load up hundreds, or even thousands, of songs on your Windows Phone, it may start to become a bit daunting trying to find content to listen to and enjoy. Thankfully, playlist support is provided so that you can easily create them on your PC and sync them over to your Windows Phone. Simply drag and drop the created playlist onto your Windows Phone icon, and the playlist and all the associated songs sync.

There is currently no support for playlist creation on the Windows Phone platform, but you can add songs to Now Playing. Now Playing is a temporary playlist that can help you select songs to play immediately, but this is not synced to your PC and is lost when you jump to play another song or album.

VIEWING DETAILED ARTIST BIOS

A cool feature of the Zune Marketplace is that you're given access to more than just the album art and songs. You can also view the entire bio of the selected artist and find out all about the artist's history and other relevant information (see Figure 7-7). To check out an artist bio, simply follow these steps:

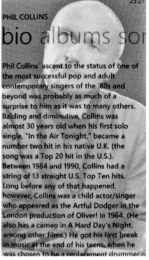

1. Select an artist in the music part of the Music & Videos hub.

2. Tap the artist's name. By default you should pop into the album tab that shows any albums for that artist you have loaded on your Windows Phone.

3. Slide you finger from left to right to view the bio. You can also slide once more across the screen to view the songs for that artist.

FIGURE 7-7 The artist bio gives you information about their career and interests.

Watching Videos

Microsoft brings the full Zune HD media experience to your Windows Phone 7 device and that includes video support. You can buy or rent the latest movies and TV show episodes and purchase music videos to watch on your PC or Windows Phone. Movie trailers are available for free; you can also receive special offers that appear in the Zune Marketplace. You can also view video content you capture on your Windows Phone and other video content you import to the Zune PC software obtained from various sources, such as a digital video recorder.

Movies can be found in the Zune Marketplace just like music; simply click the Videos tab on your PC to see available content to choose from. You cannot find video content to purchase or rent directly from the Marketplace on your Windows Phone, and a PC is required to sync the content to your device. You do this by simply dragging and dropping movie content onto your Windows Phone icon or setting up automatic sync for video content.

After you have movies on your Windows Phone, follow these steps to enjoy it:

1. Tap the Music & Videos hub from the Start screen.

2. Tap the word Videos in the list of menu items. By default, the All tab opens in the Videos area.

3. To play the video content immediately, tap the right arrow or Play icon. To find out more about the video content, tap the name of the show, movie, or video. The Play icon now appears at the bottom center of the display under the detailed description, so tap it to play.

4. Note that the video starts to play in landscape orientation, so rotate your Windows Phone to watch it (see Figure 7-8).

FIGURE 7-8 Basic video controls are large and finger friendly.

5. Video controls appear on the display for Rewind, Play/Pause, and Fast Forward. Single tap the Rewind or Forward buttons to skip in 30-second increments. Tap and hold to scroll in smaller increments. A timeline displays along the bottom to indicate where you are currently in the overall video.

6. The controls auto-hide after a couple of seconds as the show plays; to see them again simply tap the display. You can tap outside the controls on the display to hide the controls manually, too.

No on-screen volume controls exist, so use the physical Volume buttons to increase or decrease the volume of the video content.

A couple of options appear when you tap and hold on a movie, TV show, or other video content in the Music & Videos hub: Pin to Start and Delete. If you choose Pin to Start, the movie thumbnail appears on your Start screen as a single-wide tile. Tapping this tile immediately takes you into the movie player, and the content starts to play.

Enjoying Podcasts on Your Windows Phone

Podcasts are episodic audio or video content created by various people around the world. They can be localized content, such as your your favorite mobile tech enthusiast or content from major media outlets; the content is available in the Marketplace for free. Both audio and video podcasts are supported on your Windows Phone, but currently no podcasts can be discovered or downloaded directly from your Windows Phone; they must be synced from your PC through the Zune software.

When you find podcast content you want to enjoy, it is treated differently from music because you "subscribe" to the show, so you can get episodes synced to your Windows Phone as they are created and posted to the Marketplace. Shows can be daily, weekly, monthly, and so on, and the number and frequency of when you get them synced is managed from the settings on your PC in the Marketplace.

To discover podcast content in the Marketplace, follow these steps:

1. Launch the Zune PC software.

2. Click Marketplace.

3. Click Podcasts. A list of genres displays on the left with Featured, Recommended (based on your listening habits), Most Subscribed, and Newest Additions sections on the right.

4. Click a show you want to know more about. That podcast page appears with a description of the show, who the hosts are, and a list of the latest episodes.

5. If you want to listen or view a specific episode, you can right-click the show in the list of episodes and choose to download that episode.

6. If you want to get the latest episodes automatically (podcasts are managed in the settings) you should subscribe to the show. Settings include selecting how many episodes you want to download and sync to your Windows Phone.

SHARE YOUR FINDINGS WITH OTHERS The Marketplace is designed to encourage sharing and social networking. If you right-click on a podcast in the Marketplace, you see an option to share a podcast. Selecting this opens up a pop-up that gives you the ability to enter an email address and send a friend the link to the specific podcast so that they can check out the show you recommend.

After you subscribe to shows and content has downloaded to your PC, you can connect your Windows Phone and have the content synced to your device. When the content is on your Windows Phone, follow these steps to enjoy podcasts:

1. Tap the Music & Videos hub from the Start screen.

2. Tap the word Podcasts in the list of menu items. The podcast area opens up with the words Audio and Video below Podcasts showing which content is visual or audible.

3. To play the podcast content immediately, tap the right arrow Play icon. To check out a list of episodes on your Windows Phone, tap the name of the podcast. Now you can tap the name of the specific episode to find out more about the podcast, including the show notes. The Play icon now appears at the bottom center of the display under the detailed description, so tap it to play.

4. The video starts to play in landscape orientation, so rotate your Windows Phone to watch it. Audio podcasts play just like music plays, so you have on-screen controls for them as well.

5. Audio and Video controls appear on the display for Rewind, Play/Pause, and Fast Forward. Single-tap the Rewind or Forward buttons to skip in 30-second increments. Tap and hold to scroll in smaller increments. A timeline appears along the bottom of the Show icon (audio) or controls (video) to indicate where you are currently in the overall show.

If you tap and hold on the name of the show, you can choose to Pin to Start or Delete. Because podcasts are handled differently than video and music content, tapping and holding on a specific episode gives you the options to mark as Played or Delete. Marking as played is an important status because it relates to which shows are synced to your Windows Phone and helps the software keep track of what you have already listened to so that the same content is not synced to your Windows Phone more than once.

Using the FM Radio

Microsoft has minimum hardware specifications for Windows Phone devices, and one of these requirements is to have an FM radio installed in each device. The radio is integrated into the Music & Videos hub of your device. Some Windows Phone devices may also have HD FM radios where you can find better quality radio with multiple channels for some radio stations. Zune HD players all have HD FM radios.

Most Windows Phones use your wired headphones as an FM antenna, so you need to have headphones plugged into your Windows Phone to listen to radio content.

SELECTING RADIO STATIONS

After launching the FM radio, a basic user interface appears on the display of your Windows Phone (see Figure 7-9). The station number appears in large letters in the center of the display with a channel band line below the number and the station name (such as KCMS) above the station number. Up and to the left of the station name is the toggle to add or remove the station as a favorite. At the bottom of the display is a star to access your Favorites list and a central Play or Pause button.

To find stations to listen to, simply slide the channel band line right and left. If you simply flick your finger across the display, the radio seeks to the next station it can find. You can also tap the display, keep your finger on the display, and slowly slide the channel band to navigate to a specific station you want.

As you find stations you enjoy and want to tune into later, simply tap the upper-left star with a Plus icon to save it as a favorite. You can also tap and hold on the display to pin a specific station to the Start screen; this way you can quickly jump right to the station you want to hear.

FIGURE 7-9 You will see the artist and song appear on the display when listening to the radio.

LISTENING TO THE RADIO

The only control available for the radio is a simple Play or Pause button. As previously stated, you need your headset plugged in to serve as the antenna, but you can tap and hold on the display and choose speaker as the Radio mode so that you can enjoy the radio through your Windows Phone external speakers instead of using a headset.

As you listen to the radio, RDS (radio data system) technology feeds your Windows Phone the artist and song name as it plays on the station. With the Zune HD you can choose to then add this artist and song to your Zune collection, so this may be something we see in a future Windows Phone update as well.

Related Questions

✦ What is the Zune desktop software used for? **PAGE 69**

✦ Can I use Microsoft Points to buy games? **PAGE 165**

CHAPTER EIGHT

HOW CAN I VIEW, SHARE, AND CAPTURE PICTURES ON MY WINDOWS PHONE?

In this chapter:

+ Using the Pictures Hub
+ Using the Camera

Microsoft wanted to ensure that every Windows Phone was a visually stimulating and engaging device that specifies a minimal camera resolution of 5 megapixels with a flash. Every Windows Phone has the capability to capture high-quality photos and videos. It is also easy to view, share, store, and use photos and videos captured with your Windows Phone. Microsoft finds pictures so important that a double-wide tile is dedicated to the Pictures hub on your Windows Phone.

Using the Pictures Hub

The double-wide Pictures hub tile should appear by default on your Start screen; if not you can easily pin it to the Start screen. All photo content is aggregated into this hub, so you can view photos, view photo feeds and comment on photos from friends, share photos, and upload photos, and use them for background and wallpaper images on your Windows Phone.

VIEWING PICTURE GROUPS

When you first tap the Pictures hub, you see the main interface page that has group categories on the left for All, Date, and Favorites, as shown in Figure 8-1. Sliding right and left here does not take you into these sorted pages of your photos but instead shows you a couple of screens of your most recently viewed photos and a page of your photo feeds (discussed a in the Viewing Photo Feeds and Commenting section in detail).

You can customize the background image here that is shown across all four of these screens. To do so, follow these steps:

1. On the main Pictures display, tap and hold on the current background image.

2. Select Change Background or Change It for Me, as shown in Figure 8-2.

FIGURE 8-1 The first screen that appears when you tap Pictures lets you choose a photo category.

3. If you select Change Background, you can browse through the photos stored on your Windows phone. Find a photo you want to use for the background and tap it.

4. Now that the Photo Crop tool has appeared, you can slide your photo right, left, up, or down to select the area of the photo that will appear as the background.

5. When you have the area selected, tap the Crop/Check icon on the bottom of the page to apply the new background.

6. If you selected Change It for Me, the software automatically grabs an image from your collection and posts it as the background image. You can repeat this until you see an image you are happy with or do it yourself manually.

FIGURE 8-2 Tap the top options to change the background in Pictures and on your live tile.

LOCAL ONLY FOR BACKGROUNDS When you go to view photos by All, Date, or Favorites, you can find photos from the services that you subscribe to. These photos do not appear when you go to select one for your background image because only photos loading locally on your Windows Phone storage can be used for background images.

The three default picture groups are All, Date, and Favorites. If you tap All, a screen appears showing all your photos, organized into tiles labeled with names such as the following (see Figure 8-3):

+ Camera Roll (photos you took with your Windows Phone)

+ Saved Pictures (photos you downloaded and saved from your subscribed photo services)

+ Mobile Photos from Windows Live

+ Skydrive Camera Roll Photos

+ Facebook Photos in various albums set up on your Facebook account

Sliding to the right to show photos by date (you can also jump directly to here by tapping Date from the main Pictures display) shows you small thumbnails of the photos organized by month.

Sliding to the right to show photos by favorites (you can also jump directly to here by tapping Favorites from the main Pictures display) shows you small thumbnails of the photos you have identified as favorites. To set photos as your favorites, simply tap and hold on the individual photo and choose Add to Favorites. Within the Favorites page you can tap and hold a photo and remove it from Favorites as well.

FIGURE 8-3 You can view all the photos you have on your Windows Phone on one page.

VIEWING AND MANIPULATING PICTURES

In the past we often carried a number of photos in our wallet or purse to show family and friends, but now with a Windows Phone, there is no need to carry a bulky album with you to share and enjoy pictures in a fun and interactive manner. As you saw in the previous section, you know where to find the photos loaded onto your Windows Phone, so now let's check out the viewing experience.

Your photo experience is not like it used to be on a Windows Mobile device where you viewed a photo in whatever way it was presented and then used clunky methods to try to change the viewing aspects. You now have a way to view and manipulate photos using a fluid touch experience. The following techniques can be used to navigate and manipulate your photos:

+ **Scroll**: You move forward or backward through your photos by flicking. Flick from the right to left to view the next photo and flick left to right to view the previous photo.

✦ **Rotate**: When a landscape shot shows up on your Windows Phone, it gets letterboxed at the top and bottom. (This means you see black space above and below the image.) To view the photo as intended, rotate your Windows Phone 90 degrees to the right or to the left, whichever you prefer. Your photo should now fill most or all of the display. Some photos may still show black on the right and left. Similarly, if you are in land-scape orientation and a portrait-oriented photo shows up on the display, rotate your Windows Phone 90 degrees to the standard upright position to view the photo as intended.

✦ **Zoom**: Zooming is one of the slickest features of Windows Phone and one that you may be using much of the time. You can zoom in a couple of ways. There are limits to the level you can zoom as well:

  ✦ **Double tap**: As you look at a photo and want to focus in on a spe-cific area, double-tap that area to zoom in to a standard level. You can zoom in further after double-tapping using the next method. If you double-tap again, you zoom back out to the original size. You can double-tap anywhere on an image to focus on that area.

  ✦ **Spread and pinch**: To zoom in, place your fingers together on the display and spread them apart to zoom in on a specific area. You can then tap the display with them spread apart and pinch to zoom back out. Double-tapping after using the spread to zoom takes you back to the original size.

✦ **Pan**: After you zoom into a photo, you may find that you want to see other parts of that photo at the same zoom level. Simply drag your fin-ger around the display; this moves the photo with your finger so that you can focus in on other parts of the photo, which is called panning.

There are also several options for photos accessible by tapping and holding on a photo (see Figures 8-4 and 8-5). If you tap and hold on a photo, options appear that include the following:

✦ Add to Favorites

✦ Delete

✦ Upload to Facebook or Skydrive (visible option depends on your per-sonal settings)

+ Share

+ Use as Wallpaper

Favorites was discussed in the previous section, so tapping and holding on a photo is the method to add a photo to your Favorites group. You can also delete photos from your library with the Delete option. The following sections discuss Sharing and Usage options.

FIGURE 8-4 When you tap and hold on a photo you get plenty of Action options.

FIGURE 8-5 You can view and take action on photos in landscape orientation too.

VIEWING PHOTO FEEDS AND COMMENTING

When you first open up the Pictures hub and start sliding your finger right and left, you can find the Picture Groups screen, a couple of recent photos screens, and then the What's New screen. The What's New screen contains the latest photos synced from services you set up on the Accounts page that has the ability to include photos. At this time, these accounts include Windows Live and Facebook.

You can scroll up and down the What's New screen to check out photos from your contacts; when you get all the way to the bottom, you can tap Older Posts to see more photos in your feed stream. As you can see in your stream, the photo thumbnail, description, photo service, and time that the photo was shared appear on the page. Keep in mind that Windows Live supports multiple photo services, such as SmugMug and Flickr so that you can see these sources appearing in your feeds.

HOW CAN I REFRESH THESE PICTURES? You can tap and hold anywhere on the screen below the What's New title to manually refresh your photo feeds.

There are some options for interacting with the photos appearing in your feed, including viewing the full photo and reading/leaving comments (see Figure 8-6). To interact with the photo and post, follow these steps:

1. Find a photo you want to view in full, and tap the photo. The full photo appears with details on when it was shared and a comment box appearing under the photo. There may be comments already on the photo; if there are, you can read them after you open the photo as well.

2. Zoom and pan the photo as you want. There are no options for you to download the photo to your collection.

3. To leave a comment, tap in the comment box and enter text with the on-screen keyboard.

4. Tap the right Send Message icon to post your comment to the service the photo is hosted with.

FIGURE 8-6 Your friend's photos and comments appear on your Windows Phone.

HOW MANY COMMENTS ARE THERE? There may be a + or number to the right of a photo post on the What's New screen. This indicates there are comments (the number informs you how many) or a quick way to jump into the comment box so you can add your own comment.

SHARING PICTURES

Some privacy protections are in place with Windows Phone 7 so that you cannot download and save pictures from your friends' feeds and must have photos from your own services or ones taken with your Windows Phone loaded onto your device to share a photo. There are several options for sharing photos, including through Facebook or SkyDrive as a MMS, and as an email attachment.

Follow these steps to share a picture:

1. Find a photo you want to share, and tap it to open the viewer.

2. Tap and hold on the photo to see the available options appear.

3. If you want to share via Facebook, select the Upload to Facebook option from the menu. You can then add a caption to the photo while the photo uploads to your Facebook account.

4. If you want to share in another manner, select Share.

5. Select the service you want to use, and enter a message to go with the photo, as appropriate (see Figure 8-7).

Tap the Upload or Send icon to finalize the share.

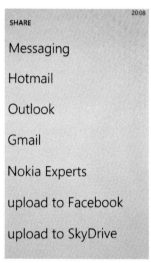

FIGURE 8-7 You can share your photos via text messaging, email, or other online services.

UPLOAD TO SKYDRIVE

It is easy to share your photos to your Facebook account because it is one of the main options in the Tap and Hold list, while also being one of the choices in the Share list. Because these Windows Phones are Microsoft products, they make uploading to SkyDrive an even easier process. SkyDrive is an online cloud sharing and storage service integrated into Windows Live. You get a 25GB account for free, and the sign-up process is handled when you first set up your Windows Live device.

Although you always have the option to share your photos with different services and accounts, you can also set up to have every photo you take uploaded to your SkyDrive account automatically and specify who can see these photos. To set this up, follow these steps:

1. Tap the upper-right Start screen arrow or slide from right to left. Tap Settings.

2. Slide your finger from right to left to view the Applications Settings page.

3. Tap Pictures + Camera.

4. Tap the right toggle bar under the words Auto Upload to SkyDrive.

5. Tap the Choose an Option drop-down list, and select from Friends, Me, Everyone (Public), or Don't Upload to cancel the action.

- -

WHERE ARE MY PICTURES GOING? By default, Facebook is selected as the service for the quick upload account, which is why it appears in the primary Tap and Hold list. Within this same Pictures + Camera settings area, you can choose to have the quick upload service be Facebook or SkyDrive. I prefer to have SkyDrive set up for automatic and Facebook as my Tap and Hold option.

- -

USE AS WALLPAPER

A few customization options are available on your Windows Phone; one is for specifying the image that appears as the wallpaper on the lock screen. You can also change the background for the Pictures hub, as detailed earlier in the sec-tion, "Viewing Pictures in Groups."

To change the lock screen wallpaper and use one of your photos for this wallpaper, follow these steps:

1. Find a photo you want to use for the background, and tap it to open the viewer.

2. Tap and hold on the photo.

3. Select the Use As Wallpaper option at the bottom of the list.

4. Pan the image around with your finger to crop it how you want it to appear where the white outlined box shows the limits of the lock screen (see Figure 8-8).

5. Tap crop when you are satisfied, and your lock screen wallpaper will be updated with this new image.

6. You can always press the physical Back button to cancel the operation.

FIGURE 8-8 There is a simple cropping tool to fit an image as wallpaper.

Using the Camera

All Windows Phone 7 devices are fitted with powerful digital cameras of at least 5 megapixels with a flash that can capture still photos and video. Microsoft also dictates that each device has a dedicated Camera Action but-ton. Manufacturers can provide cameras with higher specifications too, but Microsoft wanted to ensure that each Windows Phone owner had a reason-ably good camera experience.

CAPTURE A PHOTO FROM A LOCKED STATE

Cameras are found on most smartphones today, but to take a photo you gen-erally have to unlock the device, find the camera app and launch it, and then either tap the display or press the button to take a photo. Microsoft realized that people who have good camera phones want to just pick up the phone and capture the image, which is why a physical camera Shutter button is required. Microsoft actually gives you the ability to capture a photo while the phone is still in its locked state.

To capture a photo from the locked state, you simply press and hold the Camera Shutter button, see the camera software launch, and then press the button again to capture the photo. When you exit the camera software, these actions unlocked the device, too.

A PHONE THAT ACTS LIKE A CAMERA You can rotate your Windows Phone and capture images in either landscape or portrait orientation, but the camera software does not rotate and always remains in landscape mode.

Microsoft also studied how people reviewed photos they captured with the camera, and rather than requiring you to jump out to the Pictures hub that we talked about in the last section, you can stay within the camera application to review and manage photos and video that you captured. On the left of the viewfinder window, part of an image appears. Slide your finger from left to right to see the last photo or video you captured. You can continue flicking through these photos to see the photos you already captured. If you flick back all the way to the right, you return to the active viewfinder with the ability to capture a photo or video.

HOW CAN I GET CLOSER? You can also zoom in to your subject when capturing a photo using the + and – controls on the display. Some phones may support optical zoom, but typically they just support digital zoom. Zoom controls are also present when capturing video footage.

SHOOT A VIDEO

Windows Phone 7 cameras also support video capture capability with various resolutions supported by manufacturers. To capture a video, follow these simple steps:

1. Launch the camera software (either through a press and hold of the camera button or tapping the camera shortcut).

2. Tap the upper-right icon to switch from still mode to video mode.

3. Press the Camera button to start the recording.

4. Record your video.

5. Press the Camera button again to stop the recording.

- -

HOW LONG IS MY VIDEO? Large white numbers appear on the display while recording the video. These simply inform you how long you have been recording and do not appear on the actual video.

- -

Similar to reviewing photos you captured, you can simply slide your finger from left to right to access and play the last video you captured.

CAMERA AND STILL PHOTO SETTINGS

Some applications within your Windows Phone 7 device have settings within the application itself and also within the global settings area of the phone. This is the case for your camera, so we look at both areas to see what the minimal settings likely are for your device. Keep in mind that some manufacturers give you more control over your camera, and some of the specific settings may be different, but they will be found in the same two areas of your Windows Phone.

General Camera Settings

To access the general camera settings on any Windows Phone 7 device, follow these steps:

1. Unlock your Windows Phone.

2. Tap the upper-right arrow on the Start screen, or slide from right to left.

3. Tap Settings. You may also have pinned your settings to the Start screen; if that is the case you can just tap the Settings tile.

4. Flick your finger from right to left to access the application settings.

5. Tap Pictures + Camera.

6. You then see four toggle bars and one drop-down list. The toggle bars enable you to turn on or off the stated functionality whereas the drop-down list, talked about in the last section, enables you to set the default quick upload account. The four toggle bars give you control over the following:

+ Enable the Camera button to wake up the phone (on by default).

+ Include location (GPS) information in the pictures you take. (A prompt appears the first time you take a photo.)

+ Auto upload to SkyDrive (off by default).

+ Keep location info on uploaded pictures (on by default).

7. Tap the toggle bars to change the settings.

8. Press the Back button or Start button to leave this settings area.

The first time you take a photo or capture a video with your device, a location prompt appears to give you control over this because it is understood some people may have privacy concerns.

Local Still Photo Camera Settings

You can also find camera settings within the camera application that may vary by Windows Phone manufacturers because they are related to the camera hardware that can be different on these smartphones. The method to access and manage these settings is the same and most are self-explanatory.

To access your specific still photo camera settings, follow these steps:

1. Launch the camera application.

2. Tap the Gear icon in the lower-right portion of the viewfinder. The settings appears on the right side of the display.

3. Simply tap each setting and select from the available options. Standard settings should include the following:

+ Autofocus mode (Normal or Macro)

+ White balance (Auto, Daylight, and more)

+ Image effect (Negative, Sepia, and more)

+ Contrast (Low, High, and more)

+ Saturation (Low, High, and more)

+ Sharpness (Low, High, and more)

+ Exposure compensation (Low, High, and more)

+ ISO (Auto, 50 to 1600)

+ Metering (Average, Weighted, Spot)

+ Photo quality (Low, Medium, High)

+ Wide dynamic range (On or Off)

+ Photo resolution (dependent on camera optics)

+ Restore to default

4. After each setting is adjusted, you need to press the physical Back button to go back to the list of settings and then one more time to get out of the settings and back into the camera capture mode.

TAKING PICTURES IN THE DARK On the right as you scroll through the settings, there are icons for camera flash controls. You can simply tap one of these to enable the flash all the time, turn it off, or turn on automatic flash. You may also find that your Windows Phone 7 device has the capability for a red-eye flash.

You can optimize the quality of photos you capture by adjusting some of these settings, although the typical smartphone owner tends to leave the settings at the defaults. The final setting listed enables to you quickly return to the default settings, explore the settings to discover what settings work best for you in different environmental settings.

VIDEO SETTINGS

There are no global video settings because the camera settings discussed in the general settings may have some applicability to both video and photo content captured by the camera. There are specific video settings in the Camera application.

To access your specific video camera settings, follow these steps:

1. Launch the camera application.

2. Tap the upper-right toggle to switch into Video mode.

3. Tap the Gear icon in the lower-right portion of the viewfinder. The settings appear on the right side of the display.

4. Simply tap each setting, and select what you want from the available options. Standard settings should include the following:

   + White balance (Auto, Daylight, and more)

   + Image effect (Negative, Sepia, and more)

   + Contrast (Low, High, and more)

   + Saturation (Low, High, and more)

   + Sharpness (Low, High, and more)

   + Exposure compensation (Low, High, and more)

   + Video quality (Low, Medium, High)

   + Restore to default

5. After each setting is adjusted, you need to press the physical Back button to go back to the list of settings and then one more time to get out of the settings and back into the camera Capture mode.

There is no resolution setting and no time length control setting for your video. You should be able to capture video content for as long as you have available storage space on your Windows Phone.

SHARING AND MANAGING YOUR PHOTOS AND VIDEOS

The easiest way to access photos and videos you captured is to slide from left to right within the camera application and flick through all the content you captured. You may now want to upload, share, or delete this content. Depending on the what you specified in the global camera settings, your photos may already have been sent to SkyDrive or Facebook for sharing to others.

There is currently only one function to perform with video content because Windows Phone does not enable you to share that content. You can tap and hold on a video clip you are reviewing and choose to delete it from your collection.

For photos, you find the same available options as discussed in the Pictures hub section. If you tap and hold on a photo, options appear that include the following:

✦ Add to Favorites

✦ Delete

✦ Upload to Facebook

✦ Share

✦ Use as Wallpaper

The share options include sending via MMS or various email accounts as an attachment, upload to SkyDrive, and upload to Facebook.

You can also zoom and pan through your photos from within the Camera application.

Related Questions

✦ Can I capture a photo and use it as a lock screen wallpaper? **PAGE 1**

✦ How do I set up a Facebook account? **PAGE 57**

CHAPTER NINE

HOW CAN I READ AND USE EMAIL ON MY WINDOWS PHONE?

In this chapter:

+ Understanding the Email Interface
+ Reading and Organizing Email (Folders, Selecting, and Deleting)
+ Composing Email
+ Responding to Email
+ Email Settings

Microsoft has always been known for its powerful and functional mobile email clients, and Windows Phone devices continue this tradition of providing an extremely useful and visually appealing email application. Each email account can be pinned to the Start menu and is treated almost like a unique application. There is no unified inbox because each type of account you set up, business or personal, has a different focus.

Understanding the Email Interface

Chapter 5 discusses details of setting up your Windows Phone 7 device with various email accounts; this chapter begins by assuming that you have at least one account set up for email. Let's begin by taking a look at the standard email interface on Windows Phone 7.

To begin, first unlock your Windows Phone and tap an Email Account tile from the Start screen. At the top of the screen, you can see the account name and folder you are currently viewing. You can switch to a different folder, but the default is to start out in the inbox for the selected account (see Figure 9-1).

Below this title are four large words for All, Unread, Flagged, and Urgent. Simply flick your finger left or right across the display to switch between these different filters, and you see the contents of the email for each page change to reflect the attributes of each message. These filters offer an extremely quick method to see what emails are most important to you so that you do not have to scroll down through a long list of emails.

Taking up most of the display are the specific emails in your account. The types of information you see at a first glance include the name of the sender (largest font in the email message area), email subject, first line of the email, date sent, and an icon denoting an attachment with the email. You also see icons under the date if you took some action (replied or forwarded) on a message in your inbox.

FIGURE 9-1 When you first open an email account you will see your entire inbox.

ACCENTS INDICATE UNREAD From the main All screen of your inbox, you can tell which messages are unread because the subject of the email is colored to match the theme color you have activated on your Windows Phone.

You can quickly flick your finger up and down to scroll through your email list. Single-tapping a message opens it while tapping and holding on an email gives you options to delete, mark as read/unread, move, set a flag, or clear a flag.

At the bottom (right if you are in landscape orientation) are four icons for actions you can take with your email, as shown in Figure 9-2. These include composing a new email, viewing and switching folders, selecting an email, and syncing your email account. Tapping the More icon also gives you access to some additional email settings. (Chapter 5 discusses the primary email account settings.)

FIGURE 9-2 There are four bottom menu options and access to settings.

Reading and Organizing Email (Folders, Selecting, and Deleting)

The primary activity you will be engaged in with your email on your Windows Phone is reading email messages. After you read an email, you may want to move it to a different folder or delete it.

READING EMAIL

To read an email simply tap it and it opens in all its glory just as the sender intended. Full HTML email is supported with colorful signatures, colored fonts, and hyperlinks to email, addresses, phone numbers, websites, and more.

Windows Phone 7 has subpixel zooming support, so you can use the pinch and zoom functions seen in the Pictures hub and in Internet Explorer Mobile to enjoy your email in large fonts for those times when the standard font is just too small to read.

Let's take a look at the layout and options available to you after you tap an email to read:

+ The sender name, email subject, date and time the message was sent, and recipients are shown at the top.

+ The body of the email appears in the bottom half of the display. Touch the display and drag the message up to scroll down the email body, and you see that the body then fills up nearly the entire display.

+ Under the body you can find quick controls to reply/forward, delete, and move to the previous or next email in your inbox or selected folder.

+ You can also tap the More icon to view options for toggling the flag, marking as unread, or moving the message.

HOW ARE LARGE EMAILS HANDLED? You may find that you receive email larger than the default size that Windows Phone 7 provides, and when you get to the bottom of an email message, a note appears that you can tap to download the full message. The estimated size of the rest of the email will be shown as well.

You may also need to read email in folders other than the inbox. To switch to a different folder, take these steps:

1. Tap the Folder icon in the bottom toolbar area.

2. Tap Show All Folders if the folder you are looking for is not visible. All folders are now displayed (see Figure 9-3).

3. Tap the folder you want to view. You now see the name of the folder appear at the top of your Windows Phone display.

FIGURE 9-3 You can navigate to other folders to read your email on the go.

4. You may decide that you want this folder synced to your Windows Phone, so tap the More icon in the bottom menu area.

5. Tap Sync This Folder to include this folder in your sync actions. You can also tap the Sync icon in the bottom row. This sync setting can easily be toggled off the same way as you toggled it on.

FEEL FREE TO FILE YOUR EMAIL If you select other folders to sync to your email account, you can quickly jump between the folders by tapping the Folder icon in the bottom menu area and selecting one of the synced folders.

As you scroll to the extreme top or bottom of an email message, you see the typical Windows Phone 7 animation where the fonts are temporarily "squeezed down" to give you the sense that there is no further distance you can go.

LINKS, LINKS, LINKS Hyperlinks are associated with phone numbers, email addresses, website URLs, and physical addresses in your email body. You can tap these and actions related to the type of data will take place, such as a confirmation to place the call, opening up an address in Bing Maps, or opening up a URL in Internet Explorer Mobile. Some of these hyperlinks are not highlighted in blue or underlined, so make sure to try tapping these types of data because the intended action may still take place.

You may also receive emails with attachments, which appear between the upper email heading information and the body. The name, type, and estimated size of the attachment appear adjacent to the Paper Clip icon. Tapping the name downloads the attachment, and after it is downloaded, tapping it opens the attachment.

ORGANIZING EMAIL

Most of us do not leave email we have read and acted upon in our inbox and generally move it to another folder or delete it. There are a few ways to select, move, and delete email on your Windows Phone. To select an email for further action you can do the following:

- Tap and hold on an individual email to have a pop-up menu appear with Delete, Mark as Unread/Read, Move, and Set/Clear flag options (see Figure 9-4).

- Tap the Select icon at the bottom of the email application. This is the icon with check marks and lines to the right. After you do this, gray checkboxes appear to the left of the emails. Tapping the box places a check mark in it, so you can take action on multiple email messages (see Figures 9-5 and 9-6).

- Tap to the left of the email message and the same action that occurs when you first tap the Select icon takes place. This is a hidden function that you discover

FIGURE 9-4 There are several actions you can take on a message with a tap and hold.

FIGURE 9-5 Checkboxes appear to the left when you select email messages.

FIGURE 9-6 There are several actions you can take with selected email messages.

only after using a Windows Phone device, so show it to your friends and impress them with your vast knowledge of the operating system.

After you select email messages, you can either tap the Delete icon or choose Delete from the pop-up menu to trash the message. You can also choose to flag a message for later action or clear a flag you previously assigned. You can also choose to move the email to a selected folder. To move one or more messages perform the following steps:

1. Select one or more messages.

2. Tap the Move icon.

3. Tap the folder where you want to move the message. The message will then be moved to the folder with no further confirmation.

Composing Email

It is a fairly liberating experience to create a full email, with attachments, directly from your smartphone and conduct business from virtually any place you may be. Composing email is a primary function on your Windows Phone with an icon placed in the bottom menu bar for this function.

SMART SEARCHING OF YOUR CONTACTS As you start entering an email address in the recipient fields, your contact database is auto-filtered, and you can simply write a person's name to enter an email address. You can also choose to search the specific email directory (such as your Exchange account) for a recipient rather than entering the full email address manually.

To compose an email, perform these steps:

1. Tap an email account tile from your Start screen or thumbnail from the application shortcut screen.

2. Tap the + (Compose) icon on the bottom left of the display. The email composition form appears with the cursor placed in the To: line, as shown in Figure 9-7.

3. Enter recipient email addresses. You can also tap the + icon on the right of the To: line to choose contacts from your contact database. Multiple recipients are separated by a semicolon (;).

4. To add copy (CC) or blind copy (BCC) recipients, tap the More icon in the bottom menu area and select Show CC & BCC (see Figure 9-8).

5. Tap down in the subject line to move the cursor there, and enter an email subject.

6. Tap down into the body of the email, and use the keyboard to enter your email message.

7. To add an attachment, tap the Attach (Paperclip) icon. Currently, you can select only photos to add as attachments to your email for email messages initiated from within the email application.

8. To assign a priority level (High, Normal, or Low) to a message, tap the More icon, tap Priority, and then select a priority level.

9. Tap the Send icon to send the email message.

FIGURE 9-7 Enter an email address before jumping to the body to create your email message.

FIGURE 9-8 You can assign priorities and add additional copied recipients on your Windows Phone.

ATTACHMENTS FROM SPECIFIC APPS Although you can add only photos as attachments from directly within the email program, you can still
send attachments such as Office documents, links to your favorite songs,
and much more from within the specific application that works with these
types of information. For example, you can select to share Office documents from within the Office Mobile application.

If you change your mind while you are composing an email, you can tap the
Close icon or press the back arrow to get out of the email composition area.

Responding to Email

Although creating email from your Windows Phone is a primary activity, you
can respond to emails sent to you through your various accounts. Depending
on how comfortable you are with the keyboard on your Windows Phone, you
may find that you respond to email with short replies more than creating longer form email. Similar to the way other smartphone platforms handle email,
you must first open up the email you want to respond to. After the email is
open, take these steps to respond:

1. Tap the Respond icon in the far left of the bottom menu area.
2. Tap Reply, Reply All, or Forward.
3. If you tapped Forward, the cursor is placed in the To: line where you
   must enter a recipient.
4. If you tapped Reply or Reply All, the cursor is placed in the body of the
   email.
5. Enter an email message using the keyboard.
6. If desired, tap the Paperclip icon to add an attachment.
7. Tap the Send icon to send the email response.

You can also tap to back up into the To, CC, or BCC fields to add additional
recipients to a message you are responding to if you want to include others in
the email conversation.

Email Settings

Chapter 5 discusses specific email settings for each of the different account types, but there are also some basic settings within the email application itself. These settings are applicable to each specific account, so make sure to check each of your accounts for the settings specified.

To customize the settings for each account, take these steps:

1. Tap one of your email account tiles or shortcuts to open the email account inbox.

2. Tap the More icon in the bottom menu area.

3. Tap Settings.

4. Tap the checkbox to use an email signature, or uncheck it if you do not want to apply a signature.

5. If wanted, enter an email signature in the text entry area.

6. If you tap the Sync Settings box, you go to the settings that you specified when you set up your email account. This settings area just gives you another way to quickly access your email account settings.

Related Questions

+ How do I set up email accounts? **PAGE 57**

+ How can I send an Office document? **PAGES 173, 187, 201**

CHAPTER TEN

HOW DO I GET MORE ORGANIZED USING MY WINDOWS PHONE?

In this chapter:

+ Navigating Your Calendar
+ Adding, Editing, and Responding to Appointments
+ Viewing Multiple Calendars

A few years ago Microsoft's focus was on the PDA (personal digital assistant) where people replaced their paper planners with Pocket PCs by the thousands. One of the primary functions of a PDA was to take your calendar with you on the go; as we have moved to smartphones the last couple of years, it seems the calendar started to become less of a focus. Microsoft has a powerful personal management system for PCs with Outlook, and it took this expertise to the mobile platform with Windows Phone. As you will see, the calendar is still a focus of the mobile platform. Microsoft understands that managing our busy lives today is still a primary need, and the Windows Phone 7 Calendar is quick, simple, and effective.

Navigating Your Calendar

Microsoft understands that you need to make appointments and get help making sure you get to those appointments. Your next appointment is actually viewable and presented to you in at least three different places, so you should never miss another appointment with your Windows Phone.

You can find your next appointment appearing in these locations:

+ On the lower half of the lock screen
+ On the double wide Start screen tile
+ On the Agenda view of your Calendar

You may also consider the Day and Month views as other places where you can easily see your next appointment so there is no good excuse for missing another appointment.

To understand the Calendar, let's launch it and walk around what is visible on the display.

1. Unlock your Windows Phone.

2. Tap the Calendar tile from your Start menu or application launch screen.

3. Your Calendar launches with either the Agenda or Day mode showing (depending on what you last looked at). Simply swipe your finger right or left to switch between these views.

4. Tap the left icon in the bottom menu area to quickly jump to today.

5. You can also tap the + icon to create a new appointment or the Calendar icon to show the entire month.

6. Tapping the More icon reveals an option for managing other calendars.

DYNAMIC ICONS Did you notice that the small day and month on the Today icon is actually the correct day? This icon, like several others in Windows Phone 7, changes dynamically to help get you the best and most efficient experience possible.

Unfortunately, Calendar is one of those applications that remains in portrait orientation when you rotate your Windows Phone, so you can't see a full month in landscape. Then again, Windows Phone 7 does make good use of the portrait display with appointments for the Day and Agenda views taking up most of the display.

DAY VIEW

The Day view shows each day in 1-hour bands, labeled on the left side, as shown in Figure 10-1. As you slide your finger up the display to scroll through the day and into the next, you see the date at the top change from Today to the day of the week and date that you scroll into. This occurs with a slick animation and enhances the user experience.

FIGURE 10-1 The Calendar Day View gives you a glimpse of what is planned for the day on multiple calendars.

If you tap one of these time blocks, the new appointment screen appears, so you can create an appointment. The next section covers New Appointment creation.

- -

MULTIPLE CALENDARS SUPPORT Did you notice the different colors for the bar adjacent to the appointment and appointment title in the Day and Agenda views? These colors indicate which calendar the event is associated with; as you will read later in this chapter, you have some control over the color scheme.

- -

AGENDA VIEW

The Agenda view is similar to the Day view but gets rid of the hourly bands and presents all your appointments together with the start time in large letters, as shown in Figure 10-2. On the right you can see blocks indicating if the appointment is an all-day appointment (hollow block) or if it has a conflict with another appointment (two arrows at an angle facing each other).

A single tap on an appointment takes you into the appointment details. The details screen shows you the name, date, start and finish times, location, which calendar, reminder setting, and any note that is a part of the appointment. If you tap and hold an appointment in the Agenda view, possible options include Edit, Delete, Reply, Reply All, or Forward that selected appointment.

FIGURE 10-2 The Agenda View takes away the time context from your day.

- -

LINKS IN YOUR CALENDAR If you have an address in the location area of your appointment, you can tap it to have it mapped in Bing Maps. This hyperlinking is supported throughout Windows Phone 7, so you can have location, phone numbers, URLs, and more in the appointment notes and still single tap to open the information in the applicable program.

- -

No setting specifies what view you start in, so whatever of the two daily views (Day or Agenda) you were in last is where you will be taken when you open the Calendar. You cannot start up in Month view.

MONTH VIEW

The Month view is surprisingly more useful than you may think because you can actually see the text of your appointments for each day on the display of your Windows Phone, in large part because of the way Microsoft takes advantage of the pixels of the display. With the Month view you can quickly see what days are busy and what days may have openings, as shown in Figure 10-3. The current day is highlighted in the selected theme color of your device and tapping another day takes you directly to the day view for that specific date.

Simply slide your finger up or down to go to the next or previous month. There is currently no Week view in Windows Phone 7; however, the vivid monthly view gives you most of what you are probably looking for in a Week view layout.

FIGURE 10-3 The Calendar Month View doesn't give you much information.

Adding, Editing, and Responding to Appointments

Although creating a basic appointment can be quick and easy, several available fields in Windows Phone 7 can help you create the best event possible for you. You can edit existing events, create events with attendees, and respond to event notices sent to you.

CREATING AN APPOINTMENT

You can start creating an appointment in a couple of ways, including tapping a time band or tapping the center + icon in the bottom menu area. Initiating a new appointment is just the start though, because you have the ability to create a basic event or spend a minute or two on a couple pages of options creating the ultimate appointment.

Setting Up a Basic Appointment

The basis of an event or appointment includes answers to the questions of what, where, when, and for how long. You can find these options on the first page of the New Appointment screen; to fill these out and create this basic appointment, follow these steps, as shown in Figure 10-4:

1. From the Day or Agenda view, tap the center + icon. You can also tap a time bar in the Day view.

2. Enter a Subject for the appointment.

3. Enter a Location for the appointment (optional).

4. If multiple calendars are set up, select which account you want this appointment assigned to using the drop-down list.

5. Tap the date under When and use the Month, Day, and Year selector to specify the date of the appointment. Tap the Done button when finished.

6. Tap the Time box and use the Hour and Minute selector to specify the start time. Tap the Done button when finished.

7. Tap the box under How Long, and select from the available appointment length options. These include 0, 30, or

FIGURE 10-4 Enter some basic details to define your appointment.

90 minutes, 1 or 2 hours, All Day, and Custom. If you tap Custom, follow these steps:

A. Tap the Date box to enter the day to end the appointment. Tap Done when finished.

B. Tap the End Time box to select the time to end the appointment. Tap Done when finished.

8. Tap the Disk/Save icon to save the appointment and have it entered onto your calendar.

MAKE YOUR APPOINTMENT YOUR DESTINATION. If you add in an address for your appointment location, you can tap the location in your calendar and have Bing Maps launch with the location defined. You can then choose the location as your destination and have your Windows Phone guide you to the location.

Setting Up a Detailed Appointment

Although the basic appointments previously detailed may satisfy most of your appointment needs, there are times when you need to include more details and specifics for yourself or other attendees, as shown in Figure 10-5. Follow these steps to add more details to your appointment:

1. Complete all the previous steps for a basic appointment.

2. Tap the More Details button at the bottom of the display. Several fields appear below the end time in the New Appointment creation page.

3. Tap and select a reminder time from the drop-down list. Available notification times include 0, 1, 5, 10, 15, and

FIGURE 10-5 You can add more details to your appointment if you have a lot to cover

30 minutes, 1 hour, 18 hours, 1 day, and 1 week. There are no custom reminder times.

4. Tap the Occurs drop-down and select the frequency of the appointment. Options here include Once, Every Day, Every Weekday, Every (day of the week you have set up for the appointment), Every (day of the month you have set up for the appointment), and Every Year on the date you have set up for the appointment. There are no custom recurrence options, and you cannot create something like every Monday and Wednesday on your Windows Phone.

5. Tap the Status drop-down and select from Free, Tentative, Busy, or Out of Office.

6. To add others to your appointment/ meeting, tap the Add Someone button. You then see a display where you can add people as Required or as Optional attendees, as shown in Figure 10-6. To add people, perform the following steps:

   A. Tap the + icon to the left of Add Someone.

   B. Tap a contact from your contact list.

   C. Tap Done to leave this attendee selection page.

7. Tap the box to the left of Private if you want to keep your appointment private on the network.

8. Tap the Notes field and enter notes for the appointment onto your calendar.

FIGURE 10-6 You can add attendees as Required or Optional.

DIFFERENT LINKS ARE SUPPORTED You can enter items such as phone numbers and website URLs into your appointment notes field and then see that these turn into hyperlinks in your calendar, so you can tap and take action quickly and easily as you prepare for your appointment.

You have several options for creating appointments on your Windows Phone; these options are as extensive as you can find on any other mobile phone platform.

To edit an appointment, all the same options detailed in this section can be followed after simply tapping an existing appointment in your calendar.

RESPONDING TO AN APPOINTMENT NOTICE

You may also be invited to a meeting by a friend, coworker, or associate, and with a Windows Phone 7 device you can respond to these right from your device and continue to maintain control over your calendar. Invitations from others appear in the email inbox associated with the calendar the appointment is being sent to while also appearing in your calendar as a tentative appointment before you respond to it. The invitation appears in your calendar with stripes across the bar, compared to solid bars when you create appointments or accept them.

When an invitation arrives on your Windows Phone, take the following steps to respond from within your inbox:

1. Open the email in your inbox. The meeting invite appears with the word Invitation to start the subject.

2. Tap to open the email. You can then tap to show the calendar with the meeting invite; see the steps in the next section for details on how to handle the invite if you tap to show in the calendar.

3. Tap the right More icon to see that available options from your inbox include Respond, Delete, and Propose New Time, along with other standard email options such as Toggle Flag, Mark Unread, and Move.

4. If you tap to respond, options appear to Accept, Tentative, Decline, Reply, or Forward. Tap the action you want to take for the invitation.

5. If you tap Propose New Time, a page opens up where you can specify the new time with options to propose a Date, Time, How Long, and Add Comments to the Proposal. Fill these out and then tap the Send button to send the proposal.

6. If you tap the Delete option, the invite will be deleted and no further action is needed.

When an invitation arrives on your Windows Phone, take the following steps to respond from within your calendar:

1. Open the invitation appointment in your calendar. The meeting invite will open with two available displays for Details and Attendees.

2. Review the meeting invitation and tap an available response option. These options include Accept, Decline, Respond, and Late and they are shown as four icons across the bottom of the details page. You can also tap the three button right icon to see options for Tentative, Edit, and Delete.

3. If you tap to accept, a window appears where you can add comments and then tap Send to send the comments to the organizer. You can also choose not to send any comments and just tap Don't Send to accept the appointment into your calendar.

4. If you tap Decline, a window appears where you can add comments and then send them to the organizer. Tap Send to send the comments or Don't Send to have the appointment removed from your calendar.

5. If you tap Respond, a page of options for Reply, Reply All, Forward, and Propose New Time appear. You can take the same actions described earlier when opening the invitation in your inbox.

6. If you tap the Late icon (person running to the right) a page opens where you can choose to Text the Organizer, Email the Organizer, or Email Everyone in the attendee list.

7. If you tap the Tentative option, you have the option to enter comments in a text entry box and send the comments to the organizer along with your tentative status.

8. If you tap the Edit option, you can edit the appointment and place it on your calendar. These edits include every option you have as if you are creating a new appointment.

9. If you tap the Delete option, a confirmation box appears to verify that you want to delete the invitation.

RUNNING LATE NOTIFICATIONS Did you know that the running late functionality is present in every appointment in your calendar with attendees? You simply select the appointment and then tap the Late (person running) icon to then send a text message or email to the organizer and or attendees.

As you can see, your Windows Phone serves as an efficient personal assistant and should help you keep your appointments and respond on the go.

Managing Multiple Calendars

Part of the power of a Windows Phone 7 device is the capability to bring together several services in a single and unified user interface. As detailed in Chapter 5, a few services give you calendar syncing functionality. These services include Windows Live (calendar synchronization is loaded by default), Outlook/Exchange, and Google. (Multiple Google accounts are supported.)

WHY HAVE JUST ONE ACCOUNT? You can find support for multiple Google accounts, including email, contacts, and calendar, because Windows Phone 7 supports multiple Exchange accounts, and the Exchange ActiveSync Protocol is what Google uses for syncing this data.

You can view these multiple calendars together and can take the multiple calendars into consideration when creating appointments on your Windows Phone.

To manage various calendars on your Windows Phone, perform the following:

1. Launch the Calendar application.
2. Tap the More icon.

3. Tap the word Calendars, as shown in Figure 10-7. You then see a page open up that lists each calendar name, whether it is toggled on or off, and then shows a color for that calendar.

4. Tap the toggle bar to turn the calendar on or off.

5. Tap the color bar and then tap a color you want to use to distinguish the selected calendar from the others.

6. Press the physical Back button to back out to the Calendar.

You should then see different color appointment subject text and time bars for the appointments associated with each selected calendar.

FIGURE 10-7 It is pretty easy to access multiple calendars on your Windows Phone.

MONTH VIEW IS PRETTY WORTHLESS Unfortunately, you cannot see the different colors in the Month view and will just see small text for the appointments scheduled for the days of the week. Tap the day to see the details, including which calendar(s) the appointment is assigned to.

With multiple calendars set up on your device, notice what calendar is selected when you create new appointments, as detailed earlier. Note in the New Appointment display that there is a colored box with the word Account above it. Tap this box to select what service you want this new appointment to be created in, and make sure to check this as you create new appointments from your phone.

Related Questions

✦ How do I set up multiple accounts and calendars? **PAGE 57**

✦ How do I use Bing Maps? **PAGE 141**

✦ Can I surf the full internet with the browser? **PAGE 151**

CHAPTER ELEVEN

HOW DO I SEARCH ON MY WINDOWS PHONE?

In this chapter:

+ Bing Search
+ Voice Search Powered by Tellme
+ Search Within Applications

One of the more useful features of today's smartphones is the ability to search through the vast expanse of the Internet from the palm of your hand. Bing is growing into a popular search engine with the marketing focus on it being a "decision engine" that offers more than simple searches for terms. Bing is now an important part of Windows Phone 7 with a hardware button dedicated directly to launching it on all handsets. Microsoft purchased Tellme, a voice recognition company, a couple years ago, and we now see voice search capability integrated into one of the main hardware buttons on Windows Phone 7 as well. Lastly, you have the ability to search within several applications for data within the selected application.

Bing Search

Three main buttons appear on all Windows Phone 7 devices, and the right button is dedicated to Bing Search. It turns out that Bing Search is one of the most attractive and useful applications on your new Windows Phone device, and you will quickly discover why Microsoft dedicated a hardware button to its functionality. If you compare Bing Search on Windows Phone 7 to the way search is performed on other mobile platforms, you will clearly see that Microsoft provides you with the most integrated and fluid search experience.

Part of the attractiveness of Bing Search is its pure simplicity; to conduct a search through Bing, follow these easy steps:

1. Press the Bing Search hardware button. The beautiful Bing Search application launches with a random background image, as shown in Figure 11-1.

2. Enter a search term in the empty text box or tap the Microphone icon on the right side of the text box, and speak your search term. Notice as you enter text into the search field, Bing will auto filter and try to predict your search term to aid in

FIGURE 11-1 Note the attractive image that appears as background in Bing.

speeding up search entries. Tap in the list if you see the term you want to look for appear.

3. View the search results and tap them as you want. Selecting a search result in Web or News takes you into the Internet Explorer Mobile web browser.

LEARN WHILE YOU SEARCH What's up with the popping squares? Notice that two or more squares pop up on the Bing background image and that the image changes as you come back to the app. Tap the squares to read something about the image, including statistics, facts, and questions to ponder, as shown in Figure 11-2.

FIGURE 11-2 Interesting information is presented when you tap a square highlighted on the background image.

You see Bing Search results appear on three different screens, accessed by tapping one of the three words appearing in the now familiar metro user interface. You can find results for Web, Local, and News. Web results are the typical Internet search results you find if you were using a desktop search engine. The search term is shown in a different color font. As you scroll down the results, you can find options to see the next page of results or tap on and view related searches.

If you enter a search term for a place, whether that is a business, monument, or other location, a map appears with numbered and identified places on the Local tab of Bing Search results, as shown in Figure 11-3. A single tap on one of the places takes you directly into Bing Maps, but in a way that you won't even know you are in another application on your Windows Phone 7 device. You have options here for selecting directions, calling the location, pinning the location to the Start screen, or sharing that location via text messaging or email. You can also slide your finger from right to left to read any available reviews and slide it one more time to see businesses in the nearby vicinity of your selected destination.

News results show you any related news data associated with your search term.

FIGURE 11-3 The Local search results are identified on the map and in the list of items.

Voice Search Powered by Tellme

You can access and use search in a couple of ways by using your voice. This is extremely helpful for those times when you need to have your hands free or do not feel like typing out a long search term; the recognition is accurate and quick. I have found it to be so accurate that voice searching is my preferred method due to the speed and accuracy. The voice search part of Bing Search is powered by Tellme, a company recently purchased by Microsoft. See Figure 11-4 for the types of information you can search for with your voice.

The first way to use voice search is to tap the Microphone icon in the search entry line of Bing Search. Let's take a look at those specific steps:

1. Press the Bing Search button to launch Bing Search.

FIGURE 11-4 Wonder what you can say? Here are the answers.

2. Tap the Microphone icon in the top-right corner. A pop-up appears stating that the software is listening for your search terms.

3. Speak a search term, and give it a location or context if you want a more refined search. For example, you can say, "Movies in Puyallup, Washington" or "Find Pizza Hut in Tacoma."

4. The recognition software crunches away at both the recognition and search for your terms with a search sound and the letters alternating as the software "thinks."

5. Your search results appear on the display; you can treat them just like the search results you get with a text-based search.

Windows Phone 7 also has an amazing voice control solution, also powered by Tellme, that again is dedicated to a hardware button on your device. As discussed in Chapter 2, pressing and holding on your Start button launches the voice control software. In addition to enabling voice dialing and application launching, you can use the software to conduct Bing searches just as previously discussed.

Simply press and hold the Start button and then speak out your search term to initiate the search. The results appear, as described earlier, and you can take appropriate actions.

Search Within Applications

You can use the Bing Search button or integrated search icon, shown as a magnifying glass, to initiate searches directly within certain application databases. The applications that support context-sensitive search include email accounts (see Figure 11-5), call history, Marketplace, Maps, and People. In most other applications, pressing the Search button results in launching the Bing Search application.

Also note that the voice search functionality is not present when you initiate searches within application databases. You can use voice search

FIGURE 11-5 Watch results filter as you enter a search term.

from within the main Bing Search or voice command software enabled with the Start screen button press and hold.

Related Questions

✦ Are there settings for Bing Search? **PAGE 229**

✦ Can I search through my music collection? **PAGE 69**

CHAPTER TWELVE

HOW DO I USE GPS NAVIGATION AND MAPPING ON MY WINDOWS PHONE?

In this chapter:

+ Manage Your Location Settings
+ Control Bing Maps and Share Your Location
+ Switch Map Views and Show Traffic
+ Get Directions
+ Points of Interest (POI)

R emember when you or your dad used to stop at the gas station and ask for directions? How about when you used to print out maps and directions from your computer before you left the house in hopes that there would never be a reason to change your route? There is no reason to worry about how to get from A to B when you have your Windows Phone 7 device with you. The integrated A-GPS receiver and wireless data connection provide you with an amazing Bing Maps experience to help you find destinations, navigate to those destinations, check traffic on the way, and share your location with family and friends.

Manage Your Location Settings

Your Windows Phone device uses both the assisted GPS (A-GPS) receiver and wireless data signal to pinpoint your near exact location. A couple of areas are available to manage location settings.

WHAT IS A-GPS? A-GPS stands for assisted global positioning system and improves the startup and time to fix of your Windows Phone by using cellular and WiFi antenna triangulation to determine your position.

If location-based services are needed, follow these steps to ensure you have the best available connection:

1. Unlock your Windows Phone.

2. Slide over and down to Settings, and tap it.

3. Slide down and tap Location. The Location Settings page opens (see Figure 12-1).

4. Tap the toggle bar to turn on Location Services.

That's all there is to setting it up. There is one other setting that is specifically for the

FIGURE 12-1 Location services has just one setting.

Bing Maps service; to ensure you have the best location-based experience, turn that one on, too.

1. Unlock your Windows Phone.

2. Slide over and down to Settings, and tap it.

3. Slide the display over to Application Settings.

4. Slide down to Maps and tap it.

5. Tap the toggle bar to enable your location for local search results.

POP-UP FOR LOCATION SERVICES You also see a pop-up appear on your display when you first launch Bing Maps if Location Services are turned off, with a hyperlink to the setting to enable Location Services for more accurate navigation.

You can also choose to delete your history; tapping Delete History deletes your map searches, pins, and maps image data from your phone, as shown in Figure 12-2 There is a confirmation pop-up that appears if you tap this option before the deletions take place.

In addition to accessing the Bing Maps settings from within the general Settings area, you can also launch Bing Maps and select the settings from the bottom menu area.

Control Bing Maps and Share Your Location

Bing Maps appears to be a fairly simple application with a basic user interface and a minimal number of visible controls, as shown in Figure 12-3.

FIGURE 12-2 You can enable Location Services to achieve more accurate results with Bing Maps.

However, you can find it is also a powerful application that is quite intuitive and fun to use. After launching Bing Maps (from your Start screen or Applications screen) it takes up most of the display so that you get a viewable mapping experience.

A thin status bar appears at the top for the time and signal information with the bottom menu bar at the bottom showing three icons for directions, your location, and search. Tapping the More icon on the right pops up menu options for clearing the map, toggling the aerial (satellite) view on or off, showing traffic, or viewing the settings (see Figure 12-4).

To navigate around the map, you can perform the following gestures and actions:

FIGURE 12-3 There are a basic number of visible controls in Bing Maps.

+ Slide your finger around on your display to pan the entire map.

+ Pinch with two fingers to zoom out.

+ Spread two fingers apart to zoom in.

+ Double tap to zoom in a couple of increments, and continue to do so if you want to zoom in further. You eventually reach a point where you can no longer zoom in any closer.

+ Tap the Me icon to be taken to your current location on the map.

FIGURE 12-4 A few bottom menu items are available to control in Bing Maps.

COOL CLOSE-UP FEATURE Did you notice what happens when you zoom into the map at a certain level? The map view changes into the aerial/satellite view by default. This should be helpful for determining what your destination looks like and confirming you have reached your destination.

You can also decide to pin or share your location. Pinning your location to the Start screen lets you quickly access it again later. This is actually helpful for your home so that you can always jump right to it and choose to get directions back home after being out and about in a new location.

You may also want to share your location with family and friends. To share your location, follow these steps:

1. Either tap the Me icon to identify your location or tap and hold somewhere on the map.

2. When the black banner with the address of the location appears, tap it. Another page opens up on an About page. At the bottom are icons for Pin and Share.

3. Tap the Share icon.

4. Tap your text message account or one of your email accounts to share the location. The email or text message program appears, and the location will be pasted into the body of your email as an address.

5. Enter a recipient and send the message.

Switch Map Views and Show Traffic

You have probably used Google Maps before and experienced its map, satellite, and hybrid (map overlaid on satellite) views on the Internet. Bing Maps has two available views: Map and Aerial (aka satellite). By default Bing Maps appear in the Map view. The colors of the map are predetermined and not customizable as you find in other third-party applications.

When you enable Aerial view, you see live satellite images of the world appear with street, highway, city, and other names placed on top of the images. To toggle Aerial view on or off, follow these steps:

1. Tap the More icon in the bottom right.

2. Tap Aerial View On, and the satellite image appears.

3. Tap Aerial View Off to go back to Map view.

Zooming in to a smaller area automatically transitions you from Map view into Aerial view, as mentioned in the previous section.

Bing Maps is provided for free with a Windows Phone 7 device, and the maps are available only with a wireless data connection. One added benefit of having a wireless connection is the capability for live data to be fed into the application. Bing Maps provides you with live traffic data that is gathered from public sources, such as the Department of Transportation, and then the roads are colored to match conditions. For example, clear conditions are indicated with green lines, areas with slow traffic are in yellow, and stopped traffic appears with red lines, as shown in Figure 12-5.

Traffic data does not appear on all roads, but you should find support for traffic on the major roadways.

FIGURE 12-5 Traffic is clear in this aerial view screenshot.

Get Directions

The most powerful aspect of having a GPS receiver and mapping software is the ability to get directions to your destination. Although Bing Maps is fast, accurate, and free, it provides the same type of basic navigation that people see with Google Maps on the iPhone. This means that you get step-by-step directions, but there is no voice navigation or automatic tracking of your route as you travel. There is support for both walking and driving directions with a couple of simple icons to denote which is selected.

You can set up in Bing Maps in a couple of ways to get directions. The first way is from within the Bing Maps application. Follow these steps to set a destination and obtain directions:

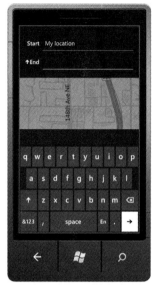

1. While in Bing Maps, tap the left-bottom icon for directions. You can also tap the More icon on the right and then tap the word Directions.

2. Enter a start location, typically selected automatically as your current location, as shown in Figure 12-6.

3. Enter a destination. The directions then appear with a small map of the first few legs with a list of each leg appearing below the map.

4. You can scroll down the list of legs and changes and tap one you want to see more of. Bing Maps zooms out and then auto-zooms back in on this selected step.

FIGURE 12-6 Enter the destination in the available text field.

5. You can also tap the Walking Person icon to switch from the default automobile directions to walking directions.

- -

DISTANCE AND ETA Did you see the distance for the entire trip, A to B, and the ETA along the top of the Map view? To the right of each leg, the specific leg distance is listed.

- -

As you travel, your position will change and track you on the map. You have to manually tap each leg in the list to track your progress because the software is not built for hands-free voice navigation at this time.

Another way to set up directions is to tap an address found through search results, in an email, on a calendar appointment, and in various other applications. Bing Maps is well integrated into the operating system so that these addresses can be tapped on to take you directly into Bing Maps. At times the address may not even be clearly identified as a hyperlink, denoted by underlined text, yet tapping it will most likely still take you into Bing Maps.

When you do find an address in another application, simply tap it. Bing Maps opens up with the address in a black flag and a pointer identifying the address. If you tap the address, you will be taken to the address-specific About page where you have options to get directions to the location, pin it to Start, or share it with others. You can also slide your finger from right to left to see what Points of Interest (POI) may be nearby on the Nearby display. Tapping one of these gives you the options discussed next.

Points of Interest (POI)

At times you may be searching for a destination that you do not have an address for, or you may just want to see what is in the local area as you travel around. As mentioned in the last section, there are two displays available for specific addresses you have identified: About and Nearby screens. Tapping the Nearby display, to the right of the About screen, presents you with a list of businesses, parks, and other locations (such as museums) that are near your destination (see Figure 12-7).

If you tap one of these, you see two available pages for this new location: About and Reviews, as shown in Figure 12-8. The About page has the following options:

❖ Specific address identified with a black flag

❖ Rating (if available)

FIGURE 12-7 Several POIs are near Qwest Field in Seattle.

FIGURE 12-8 You can view reviews, get directions, or call the destination from the About page.

- Single tap option to get directions
- Single tap option to call the location
- Ability to pin the location to the Start screen
- Option to share the location

If you slide from the About page to the Reviews page, you see a few sentences of text, the date of the review, and the star rating given by someone for that location. If you tap it, the review site opens in the Internet Explorer Mobile web browser with more details and options to leave your own review.

Related Questions

- Can I launch Bing Maps with my voice? **PAGE 15**
- Can I download and install third-party mapping solutions? **PAGE 221**
- How can I upload photos from places I visit? **PAGE 97**

CHAPTER THIRTEEN

HOW DO I SURF THE INTERNET FROM MY WINDOWS PHONE?

In this chapter:

+ Getting Started with Internet Explorer Mobile
+ Navigating to Websites
+ Working with Browser Tabs
+ Searching the Internet
+ Working with Favorites and History
+ Sharing a Web Page
+ Saving a Picture from the Internet
+ Adjusting the Browser Settings

Who would have thought a few years ago that we could walk away from any connected computer and still have full access to the world through the Internet in our pocket? With a Windows Phone 7 device and Internet Explorer Mobile, you now have that ability, with few limitations compared to your desktop web browser. Microsoft has always had a version of Internet Explorer Mobile in its Pocket PC and Windows Mobile platforms, but this latest version is based upon a hybrid-rendering engine of the IE7 and IE8 desktop browsers. The new IE Mobile browser includes features such as tabbed browsing, multitouch gesture support, a new user interface consistent with Windows Phone 7, and smooth zooming animations.

Getting Started with Internet Explorer Mobile

To launch Internet Explorer Mobile (IE Mobile), simply tap the Internet Explorer tile, as shown in Figure 13-1, or slide left to right from the Start screen, and tap the IE application shortcut. You can also find web browser hyperlinks supported throughout the operating system. For example, if you receive a text message or email with a URL included, you can simply tap the link to launch the browser.

FIGURE 13-1 The IE Mobile tile is loaded on the Start screen.

HYPERLINKS EVERYWHERE You can also find hyperlinks embedded in Office applications, Calendar appointment notes, Facebook status updates, and more, as shown in Figure 13-2. Tapping these hyperlinks launch IE Mobile by default and take you to the website URL.

Windows Phone 7 devices have accelerometers in them, so you can start using IE Mobile in either the default portrait orientation or landscape orientation. The Start and application launcher screens appear only in portrait mode, but after tapping the IE Mobile tile or shortcut, you can rotate during the launch process and start browsing in landscape orientation, as shown in Figure 13-3. That may be more familiar to you because it more closely models the desktop browsing experience. Some Windows Phone devices have slide-out QWERTY keyboards, so sliding the display up to reveal the keyboard automatically switches your orientation into landscape position, too.

Moving around within IE Mobile is quite easy and intuitive now that Microsoft has a platform with capacitive touchscreen displays and fast processors. Capacitive touchscreen displays allow you to use a finger for navigation, rather than requiring a stylus or fingernail. When IE Mobile launches and you see websites for the first time, you may see the full website appearing on the display. Even though much of it is readable, the fonts are extremely small and not in a manner you want to see when you surf the Internet. You can dynamically zoom in on what you want to read in a couple of ways:

FIGURE 13-2 Note the hyperlink embedded in a Calendar appointment.

+ Double-tap in the area you want to read, and IE Mobile zooms in so that the text in this area fills the width of the display. Double-tapping again in this area zooms you back out to the full page view.

+ Pinch and zoom on the display to zoom in to a custom level that meets your viewing needs. The text will likely not fit the column width as you zoom with this method, so you must then take your finger and slide it around the display to pan on the site.

FIGURE 13-3 Browsing in landscape orientation offers a fuller screen experience.

TRY LANDSCAPE BROWSING If you rotate your Windows Phone device into landscape orientation, as shown in Figure 13-3, you see the web page automatically adjust the fonts, on a subpixel rendering scale, to fit the display. No top or bottom text fields or menu options exist because landscape browsing is designed for full screen enjoyment of the Internet.

You can use these two methods of zooming and navigation to quickly move around the browser and read content on the different pages. Some options appear when you tap and hold on different elements of the web page, which are discussed later in the section "Saving a Picture from the Internet."

There is no quick method to jump to the top or bottom of a web page, but for pages that extend more than a single page, as you slide your finger up and down, you see a long vertical bar appear on the right side that indicates where you are on the page. You also see this bar appear on the bottom to indicate where you are horizontally, too, depending on your zoom level. You cannot tap and slide this bar; it appears only as an indicator. It auto-hides after you stop scrolling, so you can again view the entire width of the page.

USING DROP BOXES If you browse a web page with drop-down lists, tapping them opens up a full page so that you can easily select the desired text for the particular data entry field.

Navigating to Websites

Now that you have Internet Explorer up and running on your smartphone, you need to know how to navigate to different websites. As previously mentioned, you may have arrived at Internet Explorer through an embedded hyperlink and are now at a specific website. To visit a different website, you can use a few different methods for navigating links in the Internet Explorer web browser.

✛ Enter a website address (URL) manually.

1. Rotate your Windows phone to portrait orientation. The URL entry field appears at the top of the page; tap it with your finger.

2. After the keyboard appears, tap the letters to spell the website URL. You do not need to enter http://www in this entry box. There is also a .com key on the keyboard, and tapping and holding this makes the .org, .edu, and .net top-level domain suffixes appear for faster URL entry (see Figure 13-4). Microsoft has included the capability for intelligent URL entry, through Bing, and dynamically searches and provides relevant URLs as you enter them manually so that you may not even need to type the full URL and can simply tap the suggested one that appears in the list under the URL entry box.

FIGURE 13-4 If you tap and hold on the QWERTY keyboard and .COM key then other suffixes will appear for easy URL entry.

3. After spelling the URL, tap the bottom-right key (arrow pointing right) and you go to that website.

✛ Tap an embedded hyperlink on the web page you are currently visiting.

COOL KEYBOARD TRICK Instead of tapping the &123 key to enter numbers and punctuation and then tapping the abcd key to go back to letter entry, you can simply tap the &123 key, slide your finger over to the desired number or character you want to enter, and then release your finger. The selected character appears in the text field and then the keyboard automatically switches back to the mode you started with, which saves you a tap or two.

✛ Tap a Favorite or website in your history.

1. Again, rotate your Windows Phone to portrait orientation.

2. Note the Star icon on the bottom toolbar and tap it.

3. Tap one of the website titles in the list of Favorites or slide your finger from left-to-right or right-to-left to view your browsing history and tap one of those website titles.

You might also want to go back or forward as you surf the Internet on your Windows phone.

✦ To go back simply press the Back button on your Windows phone once for each page back you want to navigate.

✦ To go forward tap the More menu icon in the lower-right corner of a portrait-oriented device, and then tap forward in the list of available menu options.

MORE THAN JUST WEBSITES As you browse around the Internet, you also discover that you can tap a phone number to place a call, tap an address to map a location in Bing Maps, and tap an email address to send a message from one of your selected email accounts.

You may also be visiting a site that has fresh content posted regularly, so you can also tap the Two Arrow icon to the left of the website URL on the top toolbar to refresh the page you are visiting.

Working with Browser Tabs

People have generally moved beyond the idea of browsing on their computer in a single window, and many of us commonly have 5, 10, or even 15 open browser windows or tabs on our desktop as we multitask and search across the Internet. The concept of multiple-window-tabbed browsing has come to the mobile space as well, and all the latest and greatest mobile operating systems support tabbed browsing. Microsoft is no exception now that Windows Phone 7 is available; browsing multiple sites is quick and easy on your new Windows phone.

OPENING BROWSER TABS

The easiest way to open up a new tab in Internet Explorer is to tap the Right Central icon on the bottom toolbar, viewable only in portrait orientation, and then tap the + symbol to open up a new window/tab. There is currently a limit of six open tabs in IE Mobile, but even as a heavy mobile browser user, I have never found the need for more than six open windows on the go.

COOL TIP Did you notice that the number changes on this Tab icon on the bottom toolbar? It dynamically changes to reflect the number of open windows you have in your browser.

After you have more than one window, or tab, open, simply tap the Tab icon and then the thumbnail image of the window you want to jump into to surf that website (see Figure 13-5). It is quick and easy to jump back and forth between multiple windows using this method.

You can also open a new tab by tapping and holding on a hyperlink on a web page and selecting Open in New Tab from the available options that appear in the pop-up menu.

MANAGING BROWSER TABS

After jumping around multiple browser windows and enjoying your web browser experience, you may find that you have reached the six-tab limit. When this happens you see that the + icon is now grayed out and no longer lets you open new tabs, so now it is time to manage these tabs.

FIGURE 13-5 Several open windows in the tab browser page as thumbnails.

LIVE TABS Did you notice that the windows on the tab management display appear as small thumbnails of the page you were browsing? These are actually live browser windows, and you can see the data updated as you view these thumbnails and data changes on the web page you have up and running.

When you go to the tab display, you see a small x in the upper-right corner of each browser window. Tapping on this x closes the tab and opens up a slot for you to open up a new tab. You can close all tabs and then see there is no number in the Tab icon on the bottom toolbar. There is currently no way to view more than six browser windows in Internet Explorer Mobile.

Searching the Web

One of the primary reasons for using a web browser on a smartphone is to search for things on the go, whether that is information to answer questions, destinations you want to travel to, pricing information as you shop, and more. Two components of search use IE Mobile: searching within a web page and searching the Internet for information.

To find keywords within a web page, follow these steps:

1. Tap the More menu icon at the right on the bottom toolbar.

2. Tap Find on Page.

3. Enter a search term using the keyboard.

4. Tap Return to conduct the search.

You then see your search terms highlighted one at a time on the display with the search results highlighted in yellow and the active, selected search result highlighted in green (see Figure 13-6).

To navigate these search results, follow these steps:

1. Tap the right arrow to go to the next search result.

2. Tap the left arrow to go to the previous search results.

3. Press the Back button to jump back to the browser and get out of the search results module.

FIGURE 13-6 Web page search results appear in green and yellow highlights.

Tapping the More icon on the lower-right toolbar pops up the words Previous and Next in case you can't remember what each icon is used for.

The other search component is searching the Internet for information you need to find out more about. If you tap the Search button on your Windows Phone 7 device, you will be taken to Bing search, which enables you to search the Internet, local businesses, and news for the entered term. To search from within IE Mobile, simply enter a search term in the URL text box at the top of the page, and Bing Search shows you the results with your search term highlighted in a color that stands out from the rest of the text.

Working with Favorites and History

Entering URLs into the text box is not the most efficient way to browse the Internet, and many of us create an established list of favorite websites we like to visit on a daily basis. With a Windows Phone 7 device and IE Mobile, you can quickly jump to your Favorites and surf multiple sites with just a few taps of your finger.

SAVING A WEB PAGE AS A FAVORITE

As you browse on your Windows phone, you are likely to discover websites you enjoy and want to access in the future, so the easiest way to set these up for future visits is to add the pages as Favorites. This is a simple process, as follows:

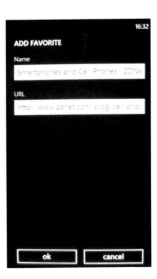

1. Rotate your Windows Phone to portrait orientation.

2. Note the + Star icon on the bottom toolbar (leftmost icon) and tap it.

3. Verify the name you want for the Favorite and the URL (see Figure 13-7). You can change the name by tapping on the text box and editing the text with the keyboard.

4. Tap OK to save the Favorite.

FIGURE 13-7 Confirm the name and URL to save a website as a Favorite.

PIN TO START MENU As cool as it is to save your most-visited websites as Favorites, it is even slicker to choose to pin these to the Start menu. Simply tap the More menu icon on the right, and choose Pin to Start to have the website shortcut added to your Start menu.

ACCESSING A FAVORITE

At the beginning of this chapter, I mentioned that you can get to a website by selecting a Favorite. To do this, follow these steps:

1. Rotate your Windows Phone into portrait orientation.
2. Tap the Star icon on the bottom toolbar.
3. Tap one of the website titles in the list of Favorites.

EDITING OR DELETING A FAVORITE

You may later decide to change the name or URL of a Favorite website or even decide to completely remove the Favorite from your device, and you can do this with a few easy steps:

1. Rotate your Windows Phone to portrait orientation.
2. Tap the Star icon on the bottom toolbar.
3. Find one of your Favorites that you want to edit or delete, and tap and hold on it.
4. A small pop-up appears; select Edit or Delete to perform your intended action.
5. If you select Edit, the name and URL appears just as if you were adding a new Favorite, so perform those same actions.

MANAGING YOUR BROWSER HISTORY

Your browser history is found in the same area as your Favorites, so tapping on the Star icon on the bottom toolbar opens up both Favorites and History. The

History page is accessed by swiping your finger right or left from the Favorites page. You can then tap a listed page in your history to visit that page or tap the Trash Can icon on the bottom toolbar to delete all your browsing history. Don't worry, a confirmation pop-up appears if you accidentally tap the Trash Can icon and didn't actually want to delete all your browser history. You cannot delete specific pages from your history, so it is all or nothing when you select to delete and clear your history.

You can also delete your history with the following steps, but be aware that this method deletes more than just your browser history. If you follow these steps, you will indeed delete your entire browser history, but you will also delete your cookies, saved passwords, and temporary Internet files.

1. Rotate your Windows Phone to portrait orientation.

2. Tap the More icon on the right on the bottom toolbar.

3. Tap Settings.

4. Tap the large Delete History button.

5. Tap Delete in the pop-up box to confirm that you want to perform this major history deletion.

Sharing a Web Page

One of the great things about having an always connected mobile device is the ability to share things with your family and friends. With IE Mobile you have the ability to share your favorite web pages in a couple of different ways.

To share a hyperlink from within a page you are viewing, follow these steps:

1. Tap and hold on a hyperlink.

2. Select Share from the pop-up menu.

3. Choose a service or account to share from. Current options include your text messaging and email accounts.

4. When your service starts up, enter one or more recipients, the subject (if sending an email), and any additional message you want to add to the shared URL.

5. Tap Send to share the web page.

To share the actual page you are viewing, follow these steps:

1. Tap the More icon on the right.
2. Tap Share from the list of menu options.
3. Choose a service or account to share from. Current options include your text messaging and email accounts.
4. When your service starts up, enter one or more recipients, the subject (if sending an email), and any additional message you want to add to the shared URL (see Figure 13-8).
5. Tap Send to share the web page.

FIGURE 13-8 The URL of the site you want to share is pasted into the body of the email.

Selecting the service will have the Windows Phone 7 operating system automatically embed the URL into the body of the email and place the entry cursor into the recipient line of the service. If you selected to share via email, you can add attachments and perform other typical email functions as well.

Saving a Picture from the Internet

While you are surfing the Internet from your Windows phone, you may run across photos you want to save for later viewing or sharing with friends. As mentioned throughout this book, the Windows Phone 7 operating system offers an integrated approach to tasks, so Internet Explorer is integrated well with the Pictures hub.

To save a picture from the Internet, simply tap and hold on the picture, and select Save Picture from the pop-up menu (see Figure 13-9).

FIGURE 13-9 Saving a picture from the Internet requires a simple tap and hold.

The picture will automatically be saved in the Saved Pictures folder in the Pictures hub on your Windows phone.

You can also tap and hold on a picture and select Share from the pop-up menu to share it with family and friends using the same sharing method previously described when sharing a web page.

Adjusting the Browser Settings

In previous versions of Internet Explorer on Microsoft's mobile platforms, quite a few available settings were on multiple pages. The settings in Windows Phone 7 are greatly simplified, and all settings are on a single page, as shown in Figure 13-10. Settings for IE Mobile include the following:

+ Allow Cookies on My Phone

+ Let Bing Suggest Sites as I Type

+ Mobile or Desktop Version website preference

+ Delete History button

If you tap the More menu icon on the right and then Settings, you see this single page of browser settings. The first two have check boxes next to them to toggle them on and off. The website preference is a round Selection button that enables you to quite easily toggle between the browser views. I previously mentioned the Delete History button; it deletes browser history, temporary Internet files, cookies, and saved passwords so you may want to use a bit of caution when using this button.

FIGURE 13-10 Browser settings all appear on one page.

Related Questions

+ How do I add a hyperlink to a Calendar appointment? **PAGE 123**

+ What is Bing Search? **PAGE 135**

+ Are there any more settings to manage? **PAGE 229**

CHAPTER FOURTEEN

HOW CAN I PLAY GAMES AND CONNECT WITH OTHERS USING XBOX LIVE ON MY WINDOWS PHONE?

In this chapter:

+ Connecting with Xbox LIVE
+ Adding Games to Play
+ Having Fun with Avatar Gadgets
+ Interacting with Your Friends

The most popular category in every mobile application store is games, and with Windows Phone 7, Microsoft demonstrates that it understands and acknowledges that people want to play games on their smartphone. Often, these games are puzzle or word games that enable you to play for 5–10 minutes and then pick up the game later to pass the time in line or while waiting for a friend. Microsoft provides support for these simple games, while also providing you with an immersive gaming experience with more advanced games. Through its Xbox LIVE service, you can take part of your console gaming experience to your Windows Phone, including managing your avatar, viewing player data, and inviting friends to play games while on the go.

Connecting with Xbox LIVE

Your Windows Phone is tied to your Live.com account, which is also associated with your Xbox LIVE account. If you do not have an Xbox LIVE account or an Xbox 360, you need to set up an account to use the Xbox LIVE gaming features. There are free (Silver) and paid (Gold) accounts. Gold accounts give you more capabilities and options for connecting with friends on a broader basis through your Xbox 360.

When you have an account associated with the Live.com account used with your Windows Phone, you see your Xbox LIVE avatar appear on your device. If you do not have an Xbox 360, you have the ability to create an avatar on your Windows Phone 7 device. You can also modify and even interact with your avatar. The avatar actually gives you a way to personalize your Windows Phone because no one will have one just like you. You can see your avatar appearing in different ways on your Start screen live tile, and if a buddy has a Windows Phone, you can identify your phones by looking at the avatars.

One of the four main displays in the Games hub is labeled Xbox LIVE, which is where you see your name, Xbox LIVE name, gamer score, and achievements. Your avatar appears on this display; this is where you can manage your avatar.

The other main displays are for the Spotlight, to view and access your game collection, and view requests to play games or invite others. See Figure 14-1 for a view showing the four main displays and how games appear on them. Use the Spotlight to highlight newly added games and let Microsoft post other important notices to all gamers.

FIGURE 14-1 There are four main displays in the Games hub on your Windows Phone and this shows you how the four are organized with multiple vertical displays.

Adding Games to Play

Although it is fun to play with your avatar, the primary reason you launched the Games hub was likely to play some games. The first display that you are launched into when you tap the Games hub from the Start screen is the Collection display where you see all the games in your collection with options to get more games from the Marketplace.

Your games appear as tiles in your Collection; to play them you simply tap the game tile. Every game is different from this point forward, so after launching the game, simply follow instructions or tap to discover all the power and functionality of the game. Some games are played in portrait orientation and some in landscape orientation with taps on the screen and even movement of the entire Windows Phone acting as control mechanisms.

Not all games are official Xbox LIVE games where you earn achievements and build up your gamer score. Many games are standalone games that you play and enjoy without building up these statistics. It is made clear in both the Marketplace and above the game tiles themselves which games are Xbox LIVE games.

As you play Xbox LIVE games, your gamer experience can increase, and you can earn achievements as you progress that are reflected in automatic updates to both your avatar and gamer tag.

To find more games to add to your collection, you can tap Get More Games on the main Games hub page. The display available in the games market include Xbox LIVE, Top, New, Free, and Categories, as shown in Figure 14-2. Tap and slide around to see all the available games. A great feature of Windows Phone is that all the priced Xbox LIVE and many of the other games can be tried out and played on your Windows Phone before you purchase them. Let's take a look at the process to buy or try a priced game on a Windows Phone:

1. Tap Get More Games. The games section of the Marketplace appears with Xbox LIVE as the first open tab.

2. Slide and tap around to find a game you want to try or buy. Tap a game tile to see more details. The game page opens up with the name, price, rating, description, screenshots, reviews, and related games all shown.

FIGURE 14-2 There are lots of available games with more showing up regularly.

3. Tap the Try button if you want to test out the game; then tap Download to download to your Windows Phone and install the game

4. Tap the Buy button if you want to purchase the game. A page opens up letting you confirm your purchase. If everything looks good, tap Buy to confirm the purchase and have the game downloaded and installed on your device.

5. After installation your game appears in the Games hub.

WHERE CAN I FIND GAMES? You can also access the games of the Marketplace right from the Marketplace hub. Tap Marketplace and then Games to go to the same area where the Get More Games link takes you.

When you open up some game tiles in the Marketplace, you see a button that lets you share that game with others because Windows Phone tries to make the gaming experience a social experience. After tapping a game in the Marketplace, take these steps to share it with others:

1. Tap the Share button.

2. Select your text message account or an email account to use for sending the game notification.

3. A text or email composition page appears with the cursor in the addressee box. You can see the subject is filled out with the body of the email consisting of the name of the game, a link to the game page from a Windows Phone, and a note on where to get a Windows Phone if the recipient doesn't have one yet.

If you start playing a game and then tap the Start button to go do something else, you can find the option to resume the game when you return because the operating system remembers where you left the game.

Having Fun with Avatar Gadgets

Your avatar is one of the main ways you have of customizing your Windows Phone to your own personality, and with the free download, mentioned in the next section, you can fully customize the avatar on your Windows Phone, as shown in Figure 14-3. That is not all that your avatar can do though, and with the free Avatar

FIGURE 14-3 My avatar is excited to be on Windows Phone 7.

Gadgets application, you can use your avatar to perform functions usually seen in standalone applications.

With Avatar Gadgets, you can have your avatar perform these functions:

✛ Interact with a bubble level on your display. Your avatar can lean and jump around as you tilt the screen while a bubble shows you the angle you are tilting your device.

✛ Your avatar can turn on and off a Flashlight tool so that you can see with your Windows Phone in the dark.

✛ Do you need to make a random decision and not have a coin available in your pocket? You avatar can flip a coin customized with the face of your avatar.

✛ Your avatar can also help you measure things with a ruler in hand.

As you can see, your avatar offers more than personalization and fun on your Windows Phone.

Interacting with Your Friends

One reason that the Xbox 360 is so popular is the ability to play games with friends across the globe. Windows Phone 7 attempts to bring some of that multiplayer feel to games through Xbox LIVE and the Games hub. As discussed earlier in this chapter, one display in the Games hub is for requests. On the Requests page, you see where you have game invites or turn notifications while also seeing the note for you to play a game and invite a friend to play with you.

If you want to play a game that supports multiplayer functionality, make sure to follow the specific game instructions for inviting players to the game. If you receive an invite or turn notification, tap it and take the appropriate action.

You can also interact with your friends from your Windows Phone in other ways. A free one-time download on your Windows Phone gives you these functions:

✛ Control and customize your avatar from your Windows Phone.

✛ See which of your friends are online and what they are doing with their console or Windows Phone.

+ Compare achievements with anybody on your friends list.

+ Communicate with anyone in the Xbox LIVE community through Xbox LIVE text messages.

The Windows Phone gaming experience is quite interactive, and as game development continues you will see new games appearing in the Marketplace on a regular basis.

Related Questions

+ Can I find games from the Marketplace hub? **PAGE 221**

+ How do I manage my wireless connections to make sure I can play against my friends? **PAGE 229**

CHAPTER FIFTEEN

HOW DO I USE WORD MOBILE 2010 ON MY WINDOWS PHONE?

One capability that has always been a part of Microsoft's mobile platforms has been the support for native Office files. Other smartphone platforms require third-party applications to edit and create Office documents; but Microsoft made Office support a central tenant of Windows Phone 7.

Word Mobile 2010 is a module in the Microsoft Office hub and is likely going to be your second most popular Office application. OneNote is likely to be in the primary spot used on your Windows Phone.

Creating a Document

Windows Phone 7 devices are designed to enable you to get things done on the go and they do their best to give you all the functionality you need when you are out and about. That said, they are not laptop replacements nor as efficient at text entry as a laptop. Some with hardware QWERTY keyboards may help you with accuracy and speed; many people are quite proficient with software keyboards, and Windows Phone 7 has one of the best available.

To create a new document on your Windows Phone, simply follow these steps:

1. Tap the Office hub from the Start screen. The Office hub may not be pinned to your Start screen; if it isn't then tap the upper right arrow to find the Office hub in the alphabetical list of applications. Office should start up in the OneNote screen.

2. Slide your finger from right to left until you see Documents on the display, as shown in Figure 15-1.

3. Tap the circle + icon to the left of the words New Document.

4. Tap Word Document from the choices available.

5. Begin entering text onto the display.

FIGURE 15-1 The Office Documents screen shows all types of Office documents, included Word documents.

LANDSCAPE WORKS WELL FOR OFFICE DOCUMENTS Don't forget that your Windows Phone has an integrated accelerometer, and by simply rotating your phone right or left 90 degrees into one of the landscape orientations, you can see a wider view of your text and get access to a larger and more comfortable QWERTY keyboard.

Several formatting options are available in Word Mobile 2010 that are discussed later in this chapter.

Saving a Document

Windows Phone handles saving your documents in a couple of ways, including locally on your device and over the Internet to your SharePoint server. Interestingly, you cannot transfer, sync, or back up documents to your PC because Microsoft is moving everything to the "cloud." The cloud is simply online storage that is supplied by another company to provide you with a safe and accessible source of storage. With the older versions of Windows Mobile, all document handling was carried out via a wired PC connection, so this is quite a departure and more in line with the latest in smartphone technology.

SAVING TO YOUR PHONE

After you finish entering text into your Word Mobile 2010 document, you can do one of two things to save your document:

+ Tap the More icon and then select Save or Save As.

+ Press the Back hardware button, and then choose Yes to save your document.

ONE FORMAT IS SAVED All Word Mobile 2010 documents are saved with the 2010 .docx extension. You may think that Save As gives you other options such as .rtf or .txt, but the Save As option is just to give you naming options and does not enable you to save in other formats.

Windows Phone 7 saves your work in progress in case you feel the need to jump out of Word Mobile 2010 and go take care of another task. When you come back to the document you were working on, you have the same two save options previously mentioned. If you come back and try to create another new document, you will be prompted to save or discard the document you were previously working on before being enabled to create a new document.

SAVING TO SHAREPOINT

If you slide to the right in the main Office Mobile 2010 hub to the SharePoint page and then select a document to download and edit, you can choose to save that document back to the SharePoint server. You can also select to keep the document for offline editing until you are ready to upload it back to the server. Version control is also supported by SharePoint.

The first thing you need to do to see the list of available documents on your SharePoint server is to enter the URL for the server by simply tapping the open URL icon and entering the URL in the text field. You may also receive emails with a SharePoint document link; then you can just tap the link to open the document from the SharePoint server.

Sharing a Document

Using the SharePoint server integration in Word Mobile 2010 may be considered one form of sharing because you and your project group work with the same folder of documents. You can share Word documents outside of SharePoint as well.

To share or send a document to someone from the main Office Mobile 2010 screens, follow these steps:

1. Tap and hold on a Word document in the list of documents.

2. Tap Send, which is one of the options shown in Figure 15-2.

FIGURE 15-2 When you tap and hold on a document you will see a few available options.

3. Select one of your email accounts to send from. You then see a compose email page open with the Word document as an attachment.

4. Fill out the compose email page with the Recipient(s), Subject, and body of the email and then tap Send.

ONE DOCUMENT AT A TIME PLEASE You cannot add multiple Word document attachments to an email. If you are in the email composition area and select Add an Attachment, you are limited to Photo Attachments only from within the email program. You must attach other documents through other applications.

To share or send a document to someone from within the document itself, follow these steps:

1. While working within a document, tap the More icon in the lower right corner.

2. Tap Send. If you have not saved the document since the last time you made changes, a pop-up appears asking if you want to save the changes before sending. Tap Yes to save your changes.

3. Select one of your email accounts to send from. You then see a Compose Email page open with the Word document as an attachment.

4. Fill out the compose email page with the Recipient(s), Subject, and body of the email and then tap Send.

From the main list of documents, you can also tap and hold on the document name to delete the document or view the properties. The properties view shows you the name, with extension, and the size of the document.

Opening and Editing an Existing Document

If you use SharePoint with your Windows Phone, you are likely to work with documents that were already created elsewhere. You may also have created documents on your Windows Phone or been sent them via email and have them saved on your device.

Attachments sent via email are handled in a slick manner because of the tight integration of Office Mobile 2010 with Windows Phone 7. You simply tap the attachment and see the document open up immediately in full-screen viewing mode with no lag or animations seen starting up an additional application; it just happens.

YOU CAN SAVE BACK IN THE SAME FORMAT Although you cannot choose which format to save documents in (the default is Word .docx), you can open up text files in a format such as .txt, .rtf, and .doc. When you finish editing, they will be saved in the same format that you opened them up in. There are limits on using the formatting tools with some text-based documents.

To open and edit an existing document from Office Mobile, follow these steps:

1. Tap the Office hub from the Start screen. Office should start up in the OneNote screen unless you have Office running and were on a different panel before.

2. Slide your finger from right to left until you see Documents on the display.

3. Tap the document you want to open. The document then opens in Viewing mode.

4. To edit the document, tap the far right Pencil (edit) icon.

5. Move the cursor to where you want to make edits, and enter text and format as you want.

You will likely find that existing Word document you open will have formatting beyond what is found natively in Word Mobile 2010. Microsoft does an excellent job of maintaining this document integrity while enabling you to perform edits. You can make edits as needed and save a document much like you started with, but also be aware there are formatting limitations in Word Mobile 2010 as detailed next.

Formatting a Document

Now that you have a good understanding of how to create, edit, and share documents, you can get into the real meat and substance of working with text in Word Mobile 2010. Word Mobile 2010 is not nearly as feature packed as the Word product you see on your PC. It does come with the essential editing tools that you are likely to use on a small screen device, and the program does a good job of maintaining existing formatting found in existing documents you want to edit.

The formatting options available to you are all found in one page of options and include styles (bold, italic, underline, strikethrough), font settings (size and color), and highlight settings, as shown in Figure 15-3. There are no options for changing the font type, inserting images, or other more advanced functions.

FIGURE 15-3 There are several formatting options in Word Mobile.

USING STYLES IN WORD MOBILE 2010

Now take a look at some of the style editing techniques in Word Mobile 2010. To work with styles, perform the following:

1. Open up an existing document or start a new document.

2. Tap the Edit icon if you are opening an existing document.

3. Tap in the document to place the cursor where you want to make edits. If you want to format a word, you can tap it to highlight the entire word. There does not currently appear to be anyway to highlight more than one word or a paragraph for formatting purposes.

4. Tap the Format icon that looks like a paint brush.

5. Tap the Bold, Italic, Underline, or Strikethrough buttons at the top of the format display to change the style of the selected text. You can also

set the style in an empty area with the cursor, and all text you enter after this spot uses the selected style until you tap Format and the Style button again to turn it off.

STICKY HIGHLIGHT Note that the selected style box stays highlighted (bold outline) in the format selection page until you tap it to toggle it off.

CHANGING FONT SIZE AND COLOR IN WORD MOBILE 2010

You can find buttons to increase and decrease font size in Word Mobile 2010. Unfortunately, no quick selector is available to jump to different font sizes, so you must tap the Increase or Decrease icon for each incremental change in font size. I counted more than 100 increments from the smallest, virtually unreadable, font size to the largest font size, so I would prefer to see a standard incremental scale drop down in a future OS update. To change font sizes, follow these steps:

1. From within a document you are creating or editing, tap a word that you want to change.
2. Tap the Format icon.
3. Tap the font Increase or Decrease icon, denoted by the letter size, and arrow up or down in the right corner.
4. Perform steps 2 and 3 repeatedly to continue to size the font as you want.

You can also find three additional font colors to choose from, including brown/orange, green, and red. Even if you have a dark theme background selected for your Windows Phone, the background in Office Mobile always appears as white, so black is the default font color. To change the font color, perform the following:

1. From within a document you are creating or editing, tap a word that you want to change.
2. Tap the Format icon.
3. Tap the font color you want to change to.

Keep in mind that you can place the cursor in one area and then enter as much text as you like with a selected color while the font color choice continues to be selected until you toggle it off.

CHANGE THE HIGHLIGHTING COLOR IN WORD MOBILE 2010

You may also want to emphasize some text in a document you are creating or editing so the ability to highlight is available. You can choose from three highlighting colors, yellow, green, and red. To add highlighting to a selected word or in a new area of text, follow these steps:

1. From within a document you are creating or editing, tap a word that you want to change.

2. Tap the Format icon.

3. Tap the highlight color you want to use.

MIX AND MATCH FORMAT STYLES You can use combinations of these formatting styles as well, so you can have bold, green, or red highlighted text. You cannot create or select from any custom color and are limited by those available in the program.

If you enabled highlighting at a cursor location rather than for a selected word, make sure to toggle off the Highlighting option when you finish highlighting in a document.

SPELL-CHECKING YOUR WORD DOCUMENT

The basic keyboard settings were discussed in Chapter 1. There were checkboxes to toggle the ability to suggest text and highlight misspelled words and correct misspelled words in areas where you enter text. Although proper spelling is important in email, text messages, and other areas where you enter text, it is often mostly thought about when you work with Word documents. I highly recommend working in Word with both of these options enabled on your Windows Phone.

As you enter words in Word Mobile 2010, the Windows Phone operating system should automatically correct your text and keep you on track for a well-spelled document, as shown in Figure 15-4. Often a word may be spelled correctly but is used in the wrong context. Microsoft suggest words, if this option is enabled, as you type, and if you see the one you want, you can tap it and move on without entering the full word. You can also go back to a correctly spelled but misused word, and Microsoft's algorithms do a great job of suggesting valid alternatives that you can simply tap to accept and enter.

If you have an unusual word or other form of the word, rather than going back with the fine cursor placement and correcting it manually, first tap the word to see what the Windows Phone OS suggests as a possible word to use. Windows Phone 7 is extremely intelligent when it comes to word usage; I haven't actually made any spelling mistakes on the device since I have been using it.

FIGURE 15-4 Microsoft includes a powerful spell checking technology in Windows Phone 7.

CURSOR PLACEMENT Windows Phone 7 provides you with fine cursor control enabling you to tap and hold in Word Mobile or a text entry field. The cursor line appears above your finger so that you can actually see it as you move it around the display to place it exactly where you want.

If a word is misspelled and doesn't get corrected, a red, squiggly line appears underneath it. You can tap the word and then choose to add it to the dictionary or have it corrected to the suggested word the operating system presents to you. If you select to add the word to your custom dictionary, the squiggly line disappears, and the word will be entered correctly the next time that you use it.

The spelling system in Windows Phone 7 is actually powerful, elegant, and accurate, and after you spend some time with it, I think you will agree.

Commenting in a Document

Although document editing and creation may not be something you enjoy doing on a small display smartphone, Microsoft makes it quite easy to review and simply add comments to a document that you can then send back to the creator for review and editing consideration. It is such a common task when working in Word Mobile that Microsoft includes a primary functional icon for it in the bottom menu area.

To add a comment to a document, perform the following steps:

1. Open up a document.

2. Switch into Editing mode by tapping the Edit (pencil) icon on the right side.

3. Tap in the document to place the cursor where you want to leave a comment, including highlighting a specific word you want to comment on.

4. Tap the Comment (conversation bubble) icon in the bottom menu bar. An empty text box appears under the selected area, as shown in Figure 15-5.

5. Enter your comment in the box.

6. Tap somewhere else in the document, or press the Back button to get back into the document.

FIGURE 15-5 Enter text into the comment box to have it assigned to the area you are reviewing.

You then see that there is a conversation Bubble icon or highlight around the word where you left a comment. You can actually leave multiple comments in the same area or throughout the document. Let's see what happens if you want to check out comments found in a document.

1. Tap a comment conversation highlight in the document. A pop-up area appears in the bottom half of the display with the initials/name of the person who left the comment and the comment itself.

2. Tap the Previous or Next arrow at the bottom of the display to read additional comments that may have been made in this area.

3. Tap the More icon and Delete Comment to remove the comment from the document.

4. Tap the Comment icon to leave your own comments.

The next and previous function applies only to the specific comments associated with the highlighted word or cursor area in the document. You need to tap each conversation comment highlight to read all the comments made in your document.

Searching Within a Document

As I have written about in a number of places in this book, search is a primary focus of the Windows Phone 7 operating system, so you expect there to be the capability to search within Word Mobile 2010. Search is simple and effective in Word with just a few steps.

1. Within a document, either in Editing or Review mode, tap the Search icon in the bottom menu area. Pressing the Search hardware button launches Bing Search and is not what you want to do at this time.

2. Enter a word to search for in the text entry box, as shown in Figure 15-6.

3. Press Enter at the bottom-right corner to initiate the search.

4. The first word found will then be highlighted.

5. Tap the Next icon in the bottom menu area to go to the next search result. When you get to the end, a pop-up box appears stating that the search is complete.

6. Tap OK to end the search.

FIGURE 15-6 Start entering a word to enable quick searching.

Navigating with the Outline Function

Microsoft includes a handy tool for quick navigation throughout a Word document that is the first icon in the lower menu area. Tapping the Outline icon can result in Windows Phone 7 automatically developing an outline of your document used strictly for quick navigation throughout the document. Follow these steps to use this handy tool:

1. Open up an existing document you created or added to your document collection.

2. Tap the Outline icon. A pop-up appears from the bottom, as shown in Figure 15-7.

3. Tap the word or phrase shown where you want to navigate in the document. The document goes to this area, and you see a preview above the pop-up area to let you check to see if this is where you want to be.

4. When you are satisfied with the area the device took you to, you can tap the document or the outline phrase again to edit or review it.

If you tap again on the Outline icon, the location you are now in will be highlighted. You can then quickly jump to another section of the document if you want.

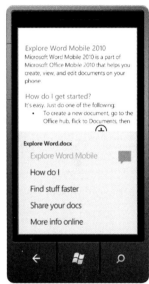

FIGURE 15-7 The outline view helps you quickly navigate through the document.

Office Mobile 2010 Settings

You should be aware of a few settings for Office Mobile 2010, and because this is the first chapter in the Office Mobile section, let's discuss them here. To access the application settings and specify what is applicable to Office Mobile, follow these steps:

1. Unlock your Windows Phone, and slide over to the application launcher page (you can also tap the upper-right arrow from the Start screen) and scroll down to Settings.

2. Tap Settings.

3. Slide your finger from right to left to view the applications settings.

4. Slide down to Office 2010 and tap Office 2010. The Office 2010 settings menu appears with settings for User Name, SharePoint, OneNote, and about.

5. Tap User Name.

6. Enter the name or initials you want to have shown for your comments and to assist with collaboration in SharePoint.

7. Tap Done.

8. Tap SharePoint.

9. Tap each setting, and enter the information as appropriate. You may need to speak with your IT department to learn what settings to enter for the UAG server. Other options include setting the data storage amount, selecting how to resolve conflicts, choosing a startup option and resetting to the default settings.

10. Press Back to go back to the main Office 2010 settings.

11. Tap OneNote.

12. Tap the toggle bar to enable or disable Automatic Sync. As we will talk about in detail in Chapter 17, you can have OneNote synced to your Windows Live/SkyDrive account and do not need a SharePoint account to use this capability.

13. Press Back to go back to the main Office 2010 settings.

14. You can tap About if you want to see what version of Office 2010 you have loaded onto your device.

Related Questions

+ How do I setup accounts to share documents? **PAGE 57**
+ Can I connect to my PC to sync documents? **PAGE 69**

CHAPTER SIXTEEN

HOW DO I USE EXCEL MOBILE 2010 ON MY WINDOWS PHONE?

In this chapter:

+ Creating a Workbook
+ Saving a Workbook
+ Sharing a Workbook
+ Opening and Editing an Existing Workbook
+ Designing and Formatting a Workbook
+ Commenting in a Workbook
+ Searching Within a Workbook
+ Navigating with the Outline Function

I am a professional naval architect and as a result I spend a fair amount of time working with Excel spreadsheets. Microsoft has always had a decent Excel Mobile program, but Excel Mobile 2010 in Windows Phone 7 is greatly improved and even includes the capability to create and display charts on your phone. It is rare to find the ability to create and edit charts on mobile plat-forms, which is just one advanced capability found in Excel Mobile 2010.

You can find many of the same formatting options in Excel that were dis-cussed in Chapter 15 for Word, but you can find more menu items in Excel than Word due to the nature of the type of data created and edited.

Creating a Workbook

Excel is a powerful program that has a large range of usefulness for people, from simple basic math calculations or budget spreadsheets all the way to multiple sheet workbooks that can help you calculate the stress and strain on a structure. Excel Mobile 2010 gives you the ability to truly take your work on the road and remain productive out of the office.

To create a new workbook on your Windows Phone, follow these steps:

1. Tap the Office hub from the Start screen. Office should start up in the OneNote screen if you were not recently running Office; if you were, it starts up on the display you were last active in.

2. Slide your finger from right to left to see the Documents on the display.

3. Tap the Circle + icon to the left of New Document.

4. Tap Excel Workbook from the available choices.

5. Begin entering text into cells, as shown in Figure 16-1.

FIGURE 16-1 Start entering formulas or data into a new Excel Mobile workbook.

SPREADSHEETS LOOK BEST IN LANDSCAPE Don't forget that your Windows Phone has an integrated accelerometer and by simply rotating your phone right or left 90 degrees into one of the landscape orientations, you can see a better layout of your spreadsheets and get access to a larger and more comfortable QWERTY keyboard.

Several formatting and functional options are available in Excel Mobile 2010 and are discussed later in this chapter. One thing to note is that you have three worksheets included in your new workbook, and you see later how to navigate between them.

Saving a Workbook

Windows Phone handles saving your workbooks in a couple of ways, including locally on your device and over the Internet to your SharePoint server. Interestingly, you cannot transfer, sync, or back up workbooks to your PC because Microsoft is moving everything to the "cloud." With the older versions of Windows Mobile, all workbook handling was carried out via a wired PC connection, so this is quite a departure and more in line with the latest in smartphone technology.

SAVING TO YOUR PHONE

After you finish entering data into the cells of your Excel Mobile 2010 document, you can do one of two things to save your document:

✛ Tap the More icon and then Save or Save As.

✛ Press the Back button, and then choose the Yes option to save your document.

ONE FORMAT TO SAVE IN All Excel Mobile 2010 documents are saved with the 2010 .xlsx extension. You may think that Save As gives you other options such as .csv, but the Save As option just gives you naming options and does not enable you to save in other formats.

Windows Phone 7 saves your work in progress in case you feel the need to jump out of Excel Mobile 2010 and go take care of another task. When you come back to the workbook you were working in, you have the same two save options previously mentioned. If you come back and try to create another new workbook, you will be prompted to save or discard the workbook you were previously working on before being enabled to create a new one.

SAVING TO SHAREPOINT

If you slide to the right in the main Office Mobile 2010 hub to the SharePoint page and then select a workbook to download and edit, you can choose to save that workbook back to the SharePoint server. You can also select to keep the workbook for offline editing until you are ready to upload back to the server. SharePoint also supports version control so that others on your team know when the document was last updated and teams do not overwrite each other's updates.

The first thing you need to do to see the list of available documents on your SharePoint server is to enter the URL for the server; you do this by tapping the open URL icon and entering the URL in the text field. You may also receive emails with a SharePoint workbook link, and then you can just tap the link to open the work- book from the SharePoint server.

Sharing a Workbook

Using the SharePoint server integration in Excel Mobile 2010 may be considered one form of sharing because you and your project group work with the same folder of workbooks, but you can share an Excel workbook outside of SharePoint as well.

To share or send a workbook to someone from the main Office Mobile 2010 Documents screen, follow these steps:

1. Tap and hold on an Excel workbook in the list of documents.

2. Tap Send, as shown in Figure 16-2.

FIGURE 16-2 When you tap and hold on a document, these options appear.

3. Select one of your email accounts to send from. You then see a compose email page open with the Excel workbook as an attachment.

4. Fill out the compose email page with the Recipient(s), Subject, and body of the email and then tap Send.

ONE ATTACHMENT ONLY PLEASE You cannot add multiple Excel workbook attachments to an email. If you are in the email composition area and select to add an attachment, you will find you are limited to photo attachments only from within the email program. You must attach other workbooks through other applications.

To share or send a workbook to someone from within the workbook itself, follow these steps:

1. While working within a workbook, tap the More icon in the lower-right corner.

2. Tap Send. If you have not saved the workbook since the last time you made changes, a pop-up appears asking if you want to save the changes before sending. Tap Yes to save your changes.

3. Select one of your email accounts to send from. You then see a compose email page open with the Excel workbook as an attachment.

4. Fill out the compose email page with the Recipient(s), Subject, and body of the email, and then tap Send.

From the main list of workbooks, you can also tap and hold on the workbook name to delete the workbook or view the properties. The properties view shows you the name, with extension, and the size of the workbook.

Opening and Editing an Existing Workbook

If you use SharePoint with your Windows Phone, you are likely to be working with workbooks that were already created elsewhere. You may also have created workbooks on your Windows Phone or been sent them via email and have them saved on your device.

Attachments sent via email are handled in a slick manner because of the tight integration of Office Mobile 2010 with Windows Phone 7. You simply tap the attachment and see the workbook open up immediately in full-screen Viewing mode with no lag or animations starting up an additional application; it just happens.

OPEN, THEN SAVE Although you cannot choose which format to save documents in (they default to Excel .xlsx), you can open up spreadsheet files in a format such as .csv. When you finish editing, they will be saved in the same format that you opened them up in. There are limits on using the formatting tools with some of these spreadsheet files.

To open and edit an existing workbook from Office Mobile, follow these steps:

1. Tap the Office hub from the Start screen. Office should start up in the OneNote screen unless you have Office running and were on a different panel before.

2. Slide your finger from right to left to see Documents on the display.

3. Tap the workbook you want to open. The workbook then opens, as shown in Figure 16-3.

4. Tap the display where you want to make edits, and enter text and format as you want.

FIGURE 16-3 You can tap on a cell and start editing an existing workbook.

PIVOT SUPPORT Excel Mobile 2010 also supports the viewing of PivotTable and PivotChart reports. You cannot create these in Excel Mobile but it's helpful that you can view them.

When you open an existing Excel file, you find that there can be many worksheets within the workbook that may have links between the worksheets and several charts. Microsoft does a great job of maintaining original formatting and design of your workbooks, and you can work in each of these worksheets and maintain that same format. When you create a new workbook you get the option for only three worksheets and you cannot add more.

ZOOM, ZOOM, ZOOM Don't forget that you can dynamically zoom out and in on your worksheets by pinching and spreading and pinching and zooming on the display with your fingers. You can also double-tap cells to jump to different zoom levels to make reading and editing your worksheet a better experience.

Designing and Formatting a Workbook

Now that you have a good understanding of how to create, edit, and share workbooks, let's work with data in Excel Mobile 2010, which is not nearly as feature-packed as the desktop Excel product you may be familiar with; however, it does come with the essential editing and creation tools that you are likely to use on a small screen device. As mentioned earlier, it is one of the most powerful mobile Excel programs available on smartphones and is included directly in the Windows Phone 7 operating system. The program also does a good job of maintaining existing formatting found in existing workbooks you want to edit.

Excel Mobile is a bit different than Word Mobile because there are design and formatting tools for the entire worksheet and tools for specific selected cells. Design tools include sorting, filtering, selecting cells, freezing panes, inserting charts, and clearing formats. You also have the ability to access and select from a large selection of functions. Formatting tools for specific cell contents include styles (bold, italic, underline, date, monetary, and percent), font colors, and fill colors. There are no options for changing the font type or other more advanced formatting functions.

DESIGN TOOLS IN EXCEL MOBILE 2010

Several options are available for designing the worksheet layouts in Excel Mobile 2010. You can access some of these through menus, some by tapping a specific worksheet icon, and some by tap-and-hold actions on the worksheet.

Tools Available in Menus

Excel Mobile has only one main menu area, which is at the bottom of your worksheet. If you tap the More icon, you find options for sorting, applying a filter, formatting a cell, inserting a chart, undoing or redoing, sending a workbook, and saving a workbook.

✦ Sort options include selecting which column to sort by and what order (descending or ascending) to use, as shown in Figure 16-4. You can also view more sort options that include secondary and tertiary sort options with the option to exclude the header row.

✦ If you tap a cell and then choose Apply Filter from the menu list, a page of possible filters, applicable to the workbook you are in, appears and you simply tap one to apply it to your selected cell(s).

✦ Formatting the cell presents you with several options that will be discussed in the next section.

✦ To activate the chart option and insert a chart, perform the following steps:

1. Tap and hold on a cell where your data for the chart begins.

2. Choose Select Cells, and scroll your finger over the cells you need selected for the chart data.

FIGURE 16-4 You can sort your columns in Excel Mobile.

3. Tap the More icon.

4. Tap Insert Chart.

5. Choose from available chart types (column, line, pie, bar, area, and xy [scatter]). Your chart will be created as a separate worksheet in your workbook.

✦ Other menu options (Undo, Redo, Send, Save, and Save As) appear in the bottom menu list as well.

NO MORE THAN THREE Although you can navigate and edit workbooks with multiple worksheets, you cannot add additional worksheets (you are given three) when you create a new workbook.

Tools Available Through Icons

Excel workbooks are generally focused on numerical data and formulas, so entering formulas is one of the most common actions taken in Excel. To access and use the formulas in Excel Mobile 2010, follow these steps:

1. Tap a cell in the worksheet. Notice that your cursor now appears in the top cell entry field with the Fx icon on the left turning black.

2. Tap the Fx icon in the upper-left corner. A list of the most common functions appears with the box for viewing more functions, as shown in Figure 16-5.

3. Tap one of the common functions or tap the More Functions box to see more; then tap a function you want to use in the cell. The function then appears in the cell entry box.

4. To carry out the action of the function, tap inside the function, and enter the cells that the function is applicable to.

FIGURE 16-5 You will find all of your most common functions in Excel Mobile.

You can also enter text or even a formula that relates to other worksheets in the cell entry box.

Tools Available Through Tap-and-Hold Actions

You can find some more global design options available to you through tap-and-hold actions on cells, columns, and rows, as shown in Figure 16-6. These include the following:

+ Cells (Select Cells, View Cell Text, Freeze/Unfreeze Pane, Merge/Unmerge cells)

+ Columns (Freeze/Unfreeze Panes, Autofit, Wrap Text, and Hide/Unhide)

+ Rows (Freeze/Unfreeze Panes, Autofit, Wrap Text, and Hide/Unhide)

As you work with each worksheet, you find clear options for all, formats, comments, and contents, so you can always go back to correct errors you make as you design and format your workbook.

FIGURE 16-6 A few options appear when you tap and hold on a cell.

FORMATTING TOOLS IN EXCEL MOBILE 2010

If you select a single cell in Excel and then tap Format, you will get access to the formatting tools. If you select multiple cells, you see the format icon, shown as a paint brush, and tapping it lets you format the cells. Formatting options in Excel Mobile include styles (bold, italic, underline, date, monetary, and percent), Font Colors, and Fill Colors, as shown in Figure 16-7.

MULTIPLE CELL SELECTION It may not be obvious, but you can select multiple cells by tapping and holding on a single cell, then dragging your finger across multiple rows and columns with the first selected cell as the base cell. You then have sort and format options to use with these cells.

Using Styles in Excel Mobile 2010

Now take a look at some of the style editing options in Excel Mobile 2010. To work with styles, perform the following:

1. Open an existing workbook or start a new workbook.

2. Tap in the workbook to select a cell or cells (selected with a tap-and-hold action) where you want to format the styles.

3. Tap the Format icon when multiple cells are selected or the More icon then Format Cell when a single cell is selected to access the available options.

4. Tap the Bold, Italic, or Underline button at the top of the format display to change the style of the selected cell. You can also tap the Date block to format the cell contents as a date, Dollar block to format the cell as a monetary value, and the Percent block to format the cell as a percentage value.

FIGURE 16-7 There are several cell formatting options in Excel Mobile.

Changing Font and Fill Colors in Excel Mobile 2010

On this same format cell page are options to change the font color or cell fill color (similar to highlighting in Word Mobile). To change the font color or fill color, follow these steps:

1. From within a workbook you are creating or editing, tap a cell or a number of cells that you want to format.

2. Tap the Format Cell icon or Format Cell menu item to access the available options.

3. Tap the font color (red, brown, or green) and fill color (red, yellow, or green) to make the change to the cell contents.

Keep in mind that the colors you select will be applied to the selected cell(s) as a whole.

Commenting in a Workbook

Although worksheet editing and creation may not be something you enjoy doing on a small display smartphone, Microsoft makes it quite easy to review and simply add comments to a workbook that you can then send back to the creator for review and editing consideration. It is such a common task when working in Excel Mobile that Microsoft includes a primary functional icon for it in the bottom menu area.

To add a comment to a workbook, perform the following steps:

1. Open a workbook.

2. Tap the worksheet to place the cursor in a cell where you want to leave a comment.

3. Tap the Comment (conversation bubble) icon on the bottom menu bar. An empty text box appears under the selected cell and above the QWERTY keyboard.

4. Enter your comment in the box.

5. Tap somewhere else in the document, or press the Back button to go back into the document.

You then see a small triangular shape in the upper-right corner of cells with comments. This triangle is colored the same as the theme you selected for your Windows Phone. You can leave multiple comments in the same worksheet but only one per cell.

Let's see what happens if you want to check out comments found in a worksheet.

1. Tap a cell with the triangular corner icon. A pop-up area appears in the bottom half of the display with the initials or name of the person who left the comment and the comment itself.

2. Tap the Previous or Next Arrow button at the bottom of the display to read additional comments that may have been made in the worksheet.

3. Tap the More icon and Delete Comment to remove the comment from the worksheet.

The Next and Previous functions take you to the next comment in the worksheet because multiple comments cannot be made in the same cell.

Searching Within a Workbook

As I have written about in a number of places in this book, search is a primary focus of the Windows Phone 7 operating system, so you expect to have the ability to search within Excel Mobile 2010. Search is simple and effective in Excel requiring just a few steps.

1. Within a workbook tap the Search icon in the bottom menu area. Pressing the Search hardware button launches Bing Search, which is not what you want to do at this time.

2. Enter a word or value to search for in the text entry box.

3. Press Enter (bottom-right corner) to initiate the search.

4. The first cell that contains the word or value found appears highlighted.

5. Tap the Next icon in the bottom menu area to go to the next search result.

6. Tap a cell outside of the search result to leave the search utility.

Navigating with the Outline Function

Microsoft includes a handy tool for quick navigation throughout an Excel document, which is the first icon in the lower menu area. Tapping the Outline icon results in Windows Phone 7 showing you the worksheets and charts in your workbook, as shown in Figure 16-8. Charts can be embedded on a single worksheet, but the outline function still indexes the charts as separate entities so that you can quickly jump to a specific chart in your workbook. Follow these steps to use this handy tool:

1. Open an existing workbook you created or added to your collection.

2. Tap the Outline icon. A pop-up appears from the bottom.

3. Tap the word or phrase shown where you want to navigate in the workbook. The utility goes to this area, and you see a preview above the pop-up area to let you check to see if this is where you want to be.

4. When you are satisfied with the area the utility took you to, you can tap the workbook above or the outline phrase again to navigate to this chart or worksheet.

FIGURE 16-8 The Outline function lets you quickly navigate throughout your Excel Mobile workbook.

WHERE IS MY COMMENT? If you have comments on worksheets, you see an icon on the right side of the outline view that indicates one or more comments are in the particular worksheet or chart.

---

5. If you tap again on the Outline icon, the location you are now in will be highlighted. You can then quickly jump to another section of the workbook using the outline utility.

Related Questions

✚ How do I set up a SharePoint server? **PAGE 215**

✚ How do I set up a new account to share my workbooks? **PAGE 57**

CHAPTER SEVENTEEN

HOW DO I USE ONENOTE MOBILE 2010 ON MY WINDOWS PHONE?

In this chapter:

+ What Is OneNote Mobile 2010?
+ Creating a Text Note
+ Adding Pictures
+ Adding a Voice Recording
+ Sharing Notes

Your smartphone is with you most of the time and serves as an important digital assistant, especially because you are probably extremely busy. Perhaps you often cannot figure out if you need to create a task, an appointment, a Word document, or an email to yourself to create your to-do list, remember that important idea that crossed through your mind, or create a shopping list for the next trip to the store. OneNote was first released on Tablet PC devices as a way to jot down your ideas and turn them into searchable repositories of your mind. Microsoft has now implemented OneNote Mobile 2010 into the Windows Phone 7 operating system to give you a lightweight version to generate some content that can later be used with the full program or as standalone information for mobile usage.

What Is OneNote Mobile 2010?

OneNote Mobile 2010 is a simple application that helps you keep track of the activities of your home, school, or work life. It is an electronic version of a sticky note and so much more. You can use it to create shopping lists, create a task list, take and store photos of business cards, and keep meeting notes. OneNote is set up to sync automatically to your Internet-based Live account, so you can always have access to your notes.

OneNote Mobile is also designed to work with SkyDrive and the basic web-based OneNote application along with your full copy of OneNote 2010 on your PC. Although you can add audio recordings and photos to your OneNote Mobile 2010 database, it isn't until you sync it to the full desktop version of OneNote that you get the ability to search for text contained within that photo. The only search capability in the mobile application involves looking through the title names.

Creating a Text Note

The handwritten note is probably the most common type of quick note that you create, but because Windows Phone 7 doesn't have handwriting support, you can capture text notes using the software or hardware QWERTY keyboard.

To create a new text note on your Windows Phone, follow these steps:

1. Tap the Office hub from the Start screen. You should start on the OneNote 2010 page, as shown in Figure 17-1.

2. Tap the + icon to the left of New Note. A blank slate opens up with the cursor in the body of the note, as shown in Figure 17-2.

3. Enter text using the QWERTY keyboard. Make sure to also tap the title area and enter a title for the note because this is how you search for notes later.

4. The three main icons give you options for numbered lists, inserting a picture, and inserting an audio clip.

5. Tap the More icon see available formatting options to add some enhancements to your text notes. You can see that options are available for Undo, Redo, Bulleted Lists, Increase Indent, Decrease Indent, and Format, as shown in Figure 17-3.

FIGURE 17-1 Office Mobile launches by default to the OneNote Mobile 2010 screen.

FIGURE 17-2 Start entering text in your new OneNote text note.

FIGURE 17-3 There are several more options in OneNote.

6. Tap format to see options for making text bold, italic, underline, or lined out, as shown in Figure 17-4. There is also a single option for highlighting parts of your note in yellow.

7. Use these formatting tools to create notes that capture your ideas and tasks.

CREATE AN OUTLINE OneNote Mobile 2010 is a handy way to create outlines for your project. Using numbered lists and increasing the indent, you can create multiple layers of text to develop an outline model.

Creating OneNote files is quite quick and easy on your Windows Phone.

Adding Pictures

In the past I used the older version of OneNote on my Pocket PC to capture objects with my camera and include photos with the notes to enhance the meaning of the notes I created. Now you can add photos to your OneNote file with the minimum specification requiring 5-megapixel cameras, which ensures many notes can include high-quality, embedded photos.

1. To add one or more photos to your OneNote file, follow these steps:

2. Tap the Office hub from the Start screen. You should start on the OneNote 2010 page.

3. Tap the + icon to the left of New Note. A blank slate opens with the cursor in the body of the note.

FIGURE 17-4 There are fewer formatting options in OneNote compared to the other Office Mobile products.

4. Enter text using the QWERTY keyboard. Make sure to also tap the title area and enter a title for the note because this is how you search for notes later.

5. Tap the Picture button in the lower menu area.

6. Browse through your photo collection to choose a photo to copy into the note.

7. If you would rather take a photo and then include it, tap the Camera icon in the center of the bottom bar.

8. Take the photo; then it appears in the note, as shown in Figure 17-5. You can add multiple photos to a single note.

9. Press the back arrow to save the note and go back to the list of notes.

FIGURE 17-5 Photos can be embedded in your OneNote document.

You can zoom in and out on the photos you embed in your notes if you want to see more detail. You can also delete the photos from your note later.

PIN TO START Did you know you can pin your OneNote notes to the Start menu? From the main OneNote page tap and hold to access the Pin to Start option. If you have a OneNote note for your latest tasks, keeping it pinned to the Start menu is a great way to keep it easily accessible for regular usage.

Adding a Voice Recording

You can create an audio recording to embed into your OneNote document. An audio recording can be a good idea for recording short meetings and ideas you have as you are out and about that you want to follow up with later. You can even capture special moments with your children in audio format.

Adding a voice recording to your OneNote file is similar to adding photos, as follows:

1. Tap the Office hub from the Start screen. You should start on the OneNote 2010 page.

2. Tap the + icon to the left of New Note. A blank slate opens up with the cursor in the body of the note.

3. Enter text using the QWERTY keyboard. Make sure to also tap the title area and enter a title for the note because this is how you search for notes later.

4. Tap the right icon (musical note with a +) to initiate the audio recording utility. You see a pop-up appear and the audio recording begins as soon as you tap the Audio icon, as shown in Figure 17-6.

5. Record your message, and then tap Stop to complete the audio recording and OK to add it to your note.

6. You then see an icon for the audio recording in your note.

FIGURE 17-6 Voice recordings can be added to your OneNote document.

You can erase the audio note, but you cannot open it up and record more to the file that was already created.

Sharing Notes

In the Office Mobile 2010 global settings, discussed at the end of Chapter 15, you can enable automatic syncing of your OneNote notes to your SkyDrive account. This syncing takes place when you open or save a note.

You may also want to share that note with someone else, so within OneNote you can email the note. To set up a note to share, perform the following:

1. Tap the Office hub from the Start screen. Navigate to the OneNote 2010 screen if you do not start there.

2. Tap an existing note you created. The note will open.

3. Tap the right icon, shown as an envelope moving to the right, to initiate sending the note.

4. Tap the email account you want to use to send the note. The note will appear as an attachment from the selected email account. The format of the notes is .one, so you need OneNote to read these notes, and the format is not universally supported.

SAVE FIRST, THEN SEND As you create OneNote notes you will find that you cannot send the note from within the creation tool. You must first finish and save your note, then open the note up as an existing file before sending to others via your selected email account.

You cannot sync OneNote files to SharePoint directly because SkyDrive is the syncing mechanism.

Related Questions

+ How do I setup a SharePoint server? **PAGE 215**
+ How do I setup a new email account to share my notes? **PAGE 57**

CHAPTER EIGHTEEN

HOW DO I USE POWERPOINT MOBILE 2010 ON MY WINDOWS PHONE?

In this chapter:

+ Opening and Navigating a PowerPoint Show
+ Editing a PowerPoint Show
+ Sharing a PowerPoint Show

There might not be many practical reasons to use PowerPoint on a display as small as shown on a mobile phone. However, there is an argument to be made for having such a program so that you can practice your presentation, make small tweaks and edits, and even project your presentation from your phone if you are a road warrior. Although you cannot create a new show on your Windows Phone, you can perform some basic editing functions. Some PowerPoint shows can also get a bit crazy with integrated animations, video, and other advanced media; these types of media are not supported in PowerPoint Mobile 2010.

Opening and Navigating a PowerPoint Show

The same technique used in Word and Excel Mobile to open an existing document applies to PowerPoint Mobile as well. Take the following steps to open a PowerPoint Mobile 2010 document:

1. Tap the Office hub from the Start screen. You should start on the OneNote 2010 page.

2. Slide your finger across the display until you see the Documents file browser. Tap directly on a PowerPoint file shown in the list of available documents.

3. If you tap and hold on the document, you see menu options for send, delete, and properties.

Properties show that readable documents have the .pptx extension. Now that you have the PowerPoint show open, what can you do with it?

- -

LANDSCAPE ONLY PowerPoint Mobile appears only in landscape orientation, but you can rotate it 180 degrees if there is a real need to do so. Keep in mind you can always pinch and zoom to read more details.

- -

To navigate within the slideshow, slide your finger up, down, left, and right on the display to browse through the slide deck. A menu on the side of the show enables you to edit, add notes, view the outline, send, and save the show.

BROADCAST SLIDESHOWS SUPPORTED You can even attend a meeting virtually from your Windows Phone. You can watch a broadcasted presentation over the Internet by tapping the compatible link that the presenter sends to you via email.

The Outline view is similar to what you saw in Word and Excel and is an extremely quick way to jump to selected slides in the show without having to scan through all of them.

Editing a PowerPoint Show

You are not going to want to spend a lot of time editing a PowerPoint deck on your smartphone. However, you may find misspelled words, a slightly different order to the presentation, and the need to add in some speaker notes as you continue to practice before you give your talk.

Follow these steps to edit a PowerPoint document:

1. Tap the Office hub from the Start screen. You should start on the OneNote 2010 page. Slide over to the Documents directly, and find a PowerPoint show you want to display.

2. Tap a PowerPoint show to open it for viewing, as shown in Figure 18-1.

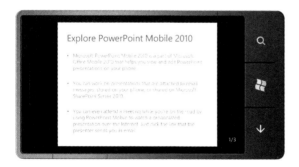

FIGURE 18-1 Review your PowerPoint slideshow in landscape.

3. Tap the Edit icon on the far right or left side. The selected slide opens in Edit mode. You can change the text on each slide, revise the speaker notes, move slides from one location to another, or hide or unhide specific slides, as shown in Figure 18-2.

FIGURE 18-2 You can perform basic editing functions in a PowerPoint slideshow.

Slide management is a handy feature of PowerPoint Mobile 2010 when in Editing mode. To move a slide, follow these instructions:

1. Tap the Edit icon.

2. Tap the option to move the slide, as shown in Figure 18-3.

3. Tap where you want it moved; then tap the check mark when you finish with the project.

FIGURE 18-3 It is easy to move slides around in PowerPoint.

Sharing a PowerPoint Show

To send a PowerPoint show to someone from the main Office Mobile 2010 documents screen, follow these steps:

1. Tap and hold on a PowerPoint show in the list of documents.

2. Tap Send from the pop-up menu.

3. Select one of your email accounts to send from. You then see a Compose Email page open with the PowerPoint show as an attachment in .pptx format.

4. Fill out the Compose Email page with the Recipient(s), Subject, and body of the email and then tap Send.

To share or send a PowerPoint show to someone from within PowerPoint itself, follow these steps:

1. While working within a PowerPoint show, tap the More icon in the lower-right corner.

2. Tap Send. If you have not saved the show since the last time you made changes, a pop-up appears asking if you want to save the changes before sending. Tap Yes to save your changes.

3. Select one of your email accounts to send from. You then see a compose email page open with the PowerPoint show as an attachment.

4. Fill out the compose email page with the Recipient(s), Subject, and body of the email, and then tap Send.

From the main list of documents, you can also tap and hold on the document name to delete the PowerPoint show or view the properties. The properties view shows you the name, with extension, and the size of the show.

You can also download PowerPoint files from your SharePoint server, use them, and then send them back for review or other uses.

Related Questions

CHAPTER NINETEEN

HOW DO I USE SHAREPOINT MOBILE 2010 ON MY WINDOWS PHONE?

In this chapter:

+ What Is SharePoint?
+ Setting Up Access to a SharePoint 2010 Server
+ Work with Documents and Information Stored on SharePoint

The newest module added to the Office Mobile 2010 suite is SharePoint, and it is well integrated into Windows Phone 7. Through SharePoint integration you obtain the ability to access documents, download them to your phone to make changes, and then save them back to the SharePoint server so that other team members can collaborate on them with you. SharePoint is commonly found in a business environment and is not a function that many consumers will use outside of the enterprise environment.

What Is SharePoint?

SharePoint is a Microsoft information and document management system that enables groups (commonly employees of a company or members of a project team) to access, share, and collaborate on document creation and editing and sharing of information and resources. SharePoint is set up on a business server and is hosted as an intranet site where you can find documents and also other information related to the company or organization hosting the SharePoint server.

SharePoint Mobile 2010 is designed to enable you to access and edit your Word, Excel, PowerPoint, and OneNote documents from your Windows Phone so that you can access them or download them for offline editing on the go, review and make changes, and sync or upload them back to the server for further editing and review by the group. You can also view other information types, as discussed later in the Information Types section.

Conflict management of documents is an important feature in SharePoint because when you download a document to edit on your phone, you are just checking out a copy, and someone else could do the same and also make edits. There is a setting for how to handle conflicts in documents that change; it is probably best to leave this set to the default manual review option.

Setting Up Access to a SharePoint 2010 Server

The first thing you need to do on your Windows Phone 7 device is enter the proper settings so that you can access the host server, aka SharePoint 2010

Server. You can access your organization's SharePoint server from within the boundaries of the company's wireless network or remotely via Microsoft Forefront Unified Access Gateway (UAG) server. To enter the proper URL and access the SharePoint server, perform these steps:

1. Tap the Office hub from the Start screen. Office should start in the OneNote screen unless you have Office running and were on a different panel.

2. Slide your finger from right to left to see the word SharePoint on the display, as shown in Figure 19-1.

3. Tap the All icon at the top of the display.

4. Tap the More icon in the lower-right corner.

5. Tap Settings. The SharePoint server settings appear on the display with options for data store, conflicts, UAG server, startup option, and reset.

6. Tap UAG server, and enter the server address, username, and password. Then tap Done.

7. Now tap the URL icon, and enter the URL for the SharePoint site, document library, list, or folder within a SharePoint site, as shown in Figure 19-2.

You can also access SharePoint through the Internet Explorer Mobile browser, but the integrated SharePoint solution in Office Mobile 2010 is easier to use and access while giving you more control over your documents

FIGURE 19-1 The SharePoint Mobile main screen appears.

FIGURE 19-2 Enter the URL for SharePoint.

Work With Documents and Information Stored on SharePoint

Now that you have your SharePoint site set up and verified, you can choose to edit and review documents directly or download them to use on your Windows Phone in offline mode. You can see there are two main SharePoint screens on your Windows Phone, one for recently accessed documents and one for recently accessed SharePoint sites. Windows Phone 7 supports the ability to access various SharePoint sites so you are not restricted to a single one.

DOCUMENTS

After you launch the Office hub and slide over to the SharePoint page you see a list of documents available that you have recently accessed. If you tap on the word All then you can view all the documents for a selected SharePoint folder, not just the most recently accessed ones that appear on the main display. Links set up within your SharePoint site are also available by sliding your finger from right to left across the display. Your company may have project folders with documents stored in different folders so the Links page will let you navigate to something like a project folder while the Documents page will show you the documents within that folder.

LINK TO SHAREPOINT Windows Phone 7 also supports access to SharePoint sites and documents that you receive links to via email. Simply tap on the URL sent to you in your email account and the Office hub will handle opening up the SharePoint site to give you access to the document.

If you tap the More icon on the documents page, you will see that you can sort documents and refresh the offline files, as shown in Figure 19-3. This is important so you can see if others are working on documents. Tap on a document to open it on your Windows Phone for editing and review. Any changes you make are automatically synced back to the SharePoint server. You can also choose to download the document for offline viewing and editing, which is important if you anticipate working in areas without a wireless connection, such as on an airplane.

If you tap and hold on a document you will see the following options:

✛ Download now

✛ Always keep offline

✛ Send link

✛ View properties

✛ Delete file on phone

You can review and edit documents just as described in Chapters 15, 16, 17, and 18. If you edit the documents or add any comments in offline mode and need to upload it to the SharePoint server, you can easily do so with your Windows Phone 7 device. After you are done editing or reviewing it, simply tap and hold to select the option to upload to the server.

If you want to share documents stored on a SharePoint server then you can use this tap and hold Send link option to share with others who have access to your SharePoint site. This is a good way to share documents with clients who have accessible folders on your SharePoint server while keeping the document integrity intact on the server. You can also download documents for offline viewing and editing and then share as described in Chapters 15, 16, 17, and 18.

FIGURE 19-3 Review the link options in SharePoint Mobile.

OTHER INFORMATION TYPES

SharePoint Mobile 2010 in the Office hub doesn't just support documents, but other information types found on a SharePoint server. For example, you may see sites/folders for announcements, reports, form templates, etc. since SharePoint is used for information exchange as well as document storage and control. Tapping on a site in the site list will show you the contents and tapping on the information will open it up so you can view and discover what is available.

Related Questions

+ How do I edit a Word document? **PAGE 173**

+ How do I edit an Excel workbook? **PAGE 187**

+ How do I edit a OneNote note? **PAGE 201**

+ How do I edit a PowerPoint show? **PAGE 209**

+ How do setup a new email account to share my documents? **PAGE 57**

CHAPTER TWENTY

WHAT OTHER APPS ARE LOADED AND HOW DO I GET MORE FROM THE MARKETPLACE?

In this chapter:

- Alarms and Calculator
- Finding New Apps in the Marketplace
- Synchronizing Apps to Your Phone
- Updating Applications

Microsoft created a fantastic new mobile operating system with Windows Phone 7 and included all the applications and utilities most people need to get things done right into the operating system. These apps and utilities include a full Office suite, full Zune media player experience, Internet Explorer web browser, Xbox LIVE games, alarm clock, calculator, and so much more. Most apps are part of hubs or are provided on the Start screen by default. Manufacturers and carriers may also have applications and utilities pre-installed on your new Windows Phone.

However, Microsoft also recognizes that people want to do even do more today with their smartphones and provides a hub dedicated to this in the Marketplace. The Windows Phone Marketplace hub offers you a way to find, select, and download apps, games, and music. The games and music parts of the Marketplace are also integrated into the Music & Videos and Games hubs.

Alarms and Calculator

Although most applications and utilities found on the application shortcut page are included in hubs or other key functions of the device, such as the camera, there are a couple of other apps loaded into the operating system by default. Although the Alarms and Calculator utilities are provided in a stock Windows Phone 7 device, you will also likely find many more applications loaded on your particular device by your wireless carrier or device manufac-turer. For example, T-Mobile includes the Slacker streaming radio application and its MobiTV solution called T-Mobile TV, whereas HTC includes its HTC Hub for people to enjoy. The HTC Hub provides access to HTC-created utilities such as a photo editor, weather application, flashlight utility, and more. AT&T includes a GPS voice guided navigation software called AT&T Navigator and a streaming radio application called AT&T Radio. Browse around your device to find all the great apps and utilities included with your purchased device.

ALARMS

You can find the Alarms utility at the top of your application Launcher screen, which is a simple utility with a single Control icon at the bottom of the display to add alarms. After you tap the Add Alarm function, you see the following options, as shown in Figure 20-1:

✚ Time of the alarm.

✚ Repeating status: Tap it to select which days you need to repeat the alarm.

✚ Sound of the alarm: Tap it to select from a list of available alarms. You can tap the Play icon at the front of the alarm sound to sample it.

✚ Name of the alarm you are setting up.

After you set up the alarm, you simply tap the Save (disk) icon to save and enable it. You then see a list of your alarms in the main Alarm panel with a quick toggle bar on the right to enable or disable the alarm. Tapping one gives you the ability to edit it or delete it.

When the alarm sounds while the display is off, a pop-up appears with buttons to snooze or dismiss the alarm. Tapping snooze silences the alarm for a 5-minute period of time.

FIGURE 20-1 Tap each box to select from the drop-down lists.

CALCULATOR

Microsoft has always included a Calculator application in its mobile operating systems, but it is nice to finally see them pay attention to this utility and make it more capable than it ever was before. When you launch the Calculator, you see a simple calculator in portrait orientation with numbers 0–9, common math functions for division, addition, subtraction, and multiplication, Plus/Minus button, Percent button, Back button, and Memory controls. Although it is basic, the buttons are nicely sized, and the two-line entry display lets you see what you entered as your first argument in the equation.

Rotating your Windows Phone into landscape orientation takes you to a scientific calculator setup with functions such as sin, cos, tan, ln. log, n!, sqrt, and more, as shown in Figure 20-2. Parentheses are available for entering more complex equations. Tapping the Pi key yields the value of Pi with 15 digits after the decimal point.

FIGURE 20-2 The land-scape calculator helps you perform advanced calculations.

Finding New Apps in the Marketplace

The Windows Phone 7 operating system focuses on the natural way you do things and the people you interact with so that tasks you want to complete are not necessarily carried out through a number of individual applications. Microsoft tried to integrate everything into a holistic experience that makes your life easier. That said, it also recognizes that many people want everything in their smart-phone, so it also provides you with the ability to discover and load up applications on your Windows Phone. The single place to visit to find applications is the Marketplace.

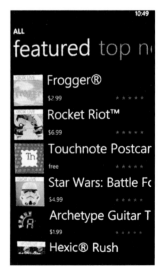

When you first tap the Marketplace hub tile, you go to the main Marketplace display that has quick links to apps, games, and music. The games and music links take you into the specific game area to shop and to the Zune Marketplace for music. These two storefronts have customized displays targeted for the specific type of content.

The main apps part of the Marketplace is where you find third-party applications to buy, try, and install. You see displays in the Marketplace for top apps, new apps, and fea-tured apps (see Figure 20-3), by category. You

FIGURE 20-3 The Marketplace has several apps available on the featured page.

can also find applications organized by categories, as shown in Figure 20-4, such as the following:

+ Games

+ Entertainment

+ Music & Video

+ Photo

+ Lifestyle

+ News & Weather

+ Finance

+ Social

+ Navigation

+ Tools

+ Business

FIGURE 20-4 The application categories are shown in this screenshot.

After you tap one of these categories, you see multiple displays available for top, new, free, and any associated subcategories. Tapping an App icon takes you to the app page that shows you the rating, description, screenshots, related apps, links to more apps by same developer, and buttons to try, buy, and share the application.

When you find an application that you want, following are the typical steps to buy or try the application and load it on your Windows Phone:

1. Find an application that you want to install.

2. Tap the application name and icon. Figure 20-5 shows the information for your selected app.

3. Tap Try or Buy for priced apps, or tap the Install button for free apps.

4. You can also decide to share the app with friends through email or SMS with a link to the store on a Windows Phone device.

FIGURE 20-5 The description, price, screenshots, and other information are shown when you select an app.

5. Confirm that you want to buy the application in the pop-up window. Buy is the option even if the app is free, too.

6. Let the app install completely; then launch it from your application launcher or Start screen.

RATE THE APP Windows Phone 7 lets you rate and review applications to help others make informed purchase decisions. Tap and hold on an application on the launcher screen to access the Rate and Review section or pin to Start (see Figure 20-6).

FIGURE 20-6 Tap and hold on Marketplace apps to pin or review them.

You see options to check the install while the app is installing, but that appears only for the period while the install is happening. After that, the application page for loaded apps shows you the Share button at the bottom so that you can share it with others.

You are only limited by the available memory on your device, so go ahead and load some applications to try them out. You can find some extremely useful applications that make your device even more powerful than it is out-of-the-box.

CAN I RUN MULTIPLE APPS AT THE SAME TIME? Windows Phone 7 supports having native apps, such as email and Zune music running actively while other apps are in use, but there are limitations on having too many apps consuming processes. Some apps are placed in a save state position so that when returning to that app, such as through the Back button, you start up right where you left off.

Synchronizing Apps to Your Phone

Similar to the way that you find music and video content on your Windows PC to sync to your Windows Phone, you can also use the desktop software to discover applications. If you are at home on your PC, it may be faster to browse through the available applications. If you find ones that you want to try or buy, simply add them to your collection. In the Zune desktop software, you simply tap Marketplace and then Apps to find applications for your Windows Phone.

You can find the Marketplace experience on the PC to be similar to that on your Windows Phone with a description, price, screenshots, and size of the application on a specific app page. After you select apps you want, the next time you connect your Windows Phone, you will find that apps can be managed just like music and videos, as described in Chapter 6.

Updating Applications

With your Windows Phone 7 device, you can discover that Microsoft takes care of application updates through the Marketplace. When a third-party application developer posts an update to the application you have loaded on your device, you will see a number appear on the Start screen Marketplace live tile.

Tapping the Marketplace tile takes you to the Marketplace main display where toward the bottom of the display you see how many application updates are available. If you tap Update, a page of app updates appears. You can tap an individual application to update it, or you can tap the Update All button to have all applications updated at once.

Related Questions

+ Where can I find out more about games? **PAGE 165**
+ Where can I learn about buying music and videos? **PAGE 83**

CHAPTER TWENTY-ONE

HOW DO I MANAGE SETTINGS ON MY WINDOWS PHONE?

In this chapter:

+ System Settings
+ Application Settings

Settings might be a rather boring topic of discussion, but it is with the settings that you can customize your Windows Phone to the optimal setup for you. Generally, after you visit and set up the settings, you don't have to revisit them too often, but when the setting is likely to be used a lot, you can find it toward the top of the display. You can find some settings within specific applications, and as mentioned throughout this book, you can quickly see if these settings are available in an application when you tap the lower-right More icon. Microsoft made setting up your device even easier by creating a single area for managing your system and application settings, so you have to dig around only a few areas for other settings on your Windows Phone.

System Settings

In general, the system settings for your Windows Phone should be fairly consistent across all devices running the Windows Phone 7 operating system. These settings include managing your sounds, wireless radios, accounts, and much more. To get to the system settings, tap the application launcher page, slide down the page to Settings, and tap Settings (see Figure 21-1).

RINGTONES & SOUNDS

One of the first things you want to do with your Windows Phone is set up the default ringtone and message alerts. Within the Ringtones & Sounds settings area, you can find toggle buttons for the Ringer and Vibration. Below these you find drop-down lists for the Ringtone, New Text Message alert, New Voicemail sound, and New Email sound (see Figure 21-2). You can also look through and tap checkboxes to play sounds for the following:

+ Appointment reminders

+ All other notifications

FIGURE 21-1 You can manage several settings in the main system Settings area.

+ Key press
+ Lock and unlock

After selecting what you want for each of these settings, simply press the Back button or Start button to leave this setting, because all settings are saved as you make the changes with no additional button to save.

THEME

Another primary way to easily customize your device is to change the background type and accent text color. In the Theme Settings area you can simply tap the Background drop-down to select from either light or dark backgrounds. The light background makes the background white with fonts in black or accent colors. The dark background turns the background black, and fonts appear in white and accent colors.

FIGURE 21-2 Customize your ringer and alarm sounds with this Settings page.

Tapping the Accent Color drop-down gives you options to select from a number of colors, including teal, lime, brown, orange, blue, red, and green. I have personally found the dark background with brown accent color to be my favorite.

AIRPLANE MODE

The Airplane Mode setting is one of those that you may actually visit more than once, and like the Ringtone and Theme settings is found toward the top of the Settings page. This setting is basic and enables you simply tap a toggle bar to turn off your cellular, Wi-Fi, and Bluetooth radios for traveling on an airplane. You can actually turn on Wi-Fi and Bluetooth radios later in case you happen to be on an airplane with Wi-Fi support.

WI-FI

The Wi-Fi setting has a toggle to turn on or off the Wi-Fi radio, and as just stated, you can enable this in Airplane Mode, if needed. There is a checkbox that you can select to have your Windows Phone notify you when a new wire-less network is available. When a new one is in range, a notification appears at the top of your Windows Phone so that you can manage if you want to con-nect to it.

On the bottom half of the Wi-Fi settings display, you can manage the net-works you have connections set up with, including entering needed security settings.

BLUETOOTH

Again we see that wireless management settings are toward the top of the system Settings page, and in this case you have the toggle for the Bluetooth radio. The details of connecting to devices were discussed in Chapter 3. The Bluetooth settings enable you to manage your Bluetooth devices and connections.

EMAIL & ACCOUNTS

The Email & Accounts settings give you the ability to add new accounts and manage existing account settings. This ability was discussed in great detail in Chapter 5 because different accounts have different settings, based on what type of data synchronization is supported.

LOCK & WALLPAPER

You manage your Lock screen settings through the Lock & Wallpaper option. This setting was discussed in detail in Chapter 2 and is one you will want to set up early because the Lock screen is something you interact with quite often, and you want a nice wallpaper available to view.

LOCATION

Several applications, primarily Bing Search and Bing Maps, are enhanced by knowing your location. In this setting you can toggle on or off the Global Location settings services.

CELLULAR

Windows Phone 7 does a great job to make sure your Cellular settings are taken care of automatically, but you may find that you need some manual control over your Cellular settings when you travel outside of your home area. Within the Cellular settings you have options for toggling on or off your Data Connection, setting Data Roaming options, and entering an access point manually. Watch your Data Roaming settings when traveling, or you may end up with some high cellular phone bills.

DATE & TIME

You have two simple toggle bars for the Date & Time settings; in most cases you have the ability to have the date and time set automatically. If you do not want your cellular provider to keep your Windows Phone time and date updated, you can turn off the option. If you do this, you see drop-down lists for Time, Date, and Time Zone.

There is also a toggle bar to enable the 24-hour clock function. As a veteran military officer, I prefer to use this 24-hour clock format on my devices.

BRIGHTNESS

By default, your display brightness is set to automatically adjust for optimal performance, and in all likelihood you will be satisfied with the setting. If you want to manually manage your screen brightness, you can toggle the Automatic setting to off and then use the Level drop-down list to choose from Low, Medium, or High. Keep in mind that the brighter your display is, the more battery power you consume.

KEYBOARD

The keyboard on your Windows Phone 7 device is good at helping you enter text accurately, and with these keyboard settings you have even more control over how this is handled. The following keyboard settings are available on your Windows Phone, as shown in Figure 21-3:

✦ Suggest Text and Highlight Misspelled Words.

+ Correct Misspelled Words.

+ Insert a Space After Selecting a Suggestion.

+ Insert a Period after Double-Tapping the Spacebar.

+ Capitalize the First Letter of a Sentence.

As discussed in more detail in Chapter 2, the keyboard offers a first-rate text entry experience, and you should do quite well with text entry with a bit of practice.

Depending on your particular Windows Phone device, you may be able to select a keyboard in a different language using the drop-down list.

FIGURE 21-3 Check the boxes next to those options you want enabled for your keyboard.

REGION & LANGUAGE

The Region and Language options will be dependent on what is provided for you on your phone by your carrier or manufacturer. Some of the changes require a phone restart because the language is a central base upon which menus, tiles, and every text field is based upon. With a selected language you can find options for region formats using the drop-down list.

You can also select how you want the short and long dates on your device to appear. The desired first day of the week is customizable in case you happen to work a nontraditional work week. Even the browser and search language can be specifically identified on your Windows Phone.

EASE OF ACCESS

Microsoft provides settings for TTY/TDD mode. TTY (telephone typewriter) or TDD (telecommunications device for the deaf) mode is used to assist those with hearing impairments use a Windows Phone 7 smartphone. Options for TTY/TDD mode include the following:

+ Off

+ Full

+ HCO (hearing carry over)

+ VCO (voice carry over)

After selecting the option you want, you simply press the Back button to go back into the System settings area or the Start button to get back to the main display.

SPEECH

When you press and hold the Start button, the Speech utility appears where you can perform voice controls of your device via audio commands. In the Speech settings area, you can select to Play Audio Confirmations, Use Speech When the Phone is Locked, and Enable Speech Recognition over the Network, as shown in Figure 21-4.

If you select to have speech enabled when the phone is locked, a press and hold of the Start button launches the Speech utility, powered by Tellme technology, so you can control your phone without even sliding up the Lock screen wallpaper. You do have to first turn on the display, which prevents accidental activation with a button press in your pocket.

To conduct web searches using your voice, you need to make sure to have the speech recognition over the network enabled. This also sends voice commands to Microsoft to use to help improve this service.

FIGURE 21-4 It is handy to have Speech enabled when the phone is locked.

FIND MY PHONE

One of the major reasons to set up a Windows Live account on your Windows Phone (see Chapter 5) is to have access to the free Find My Phone service that Live.com provides to you. With this service enabled on your Windows Phone, you can map, ring, lock, or erase your phone—all from within a web browser accessible from anywhere.

The cool thing about the ability to ring and find your phone is that it will force a unique ring of your Windows Phone even if you last had it with vibration mode enabled. Some of my family members are always misplacing their phone, so this ability to find the phone from a web browser Control Panel is invaluable.

If you discover that your phone was not misplaced but was actually stolen, you can try to map its location. You should not attempt to recover it yourself, though, if it were stolen and should notify the police to handle the situation. For security reasons, you can also choose to lock your phone or completely erase it and wipe it clean if there is no chance of recovery. Someone may have found it in a bar or some other place, so sending them a message or calling your phone might result in its safe return from an honest finder.

After first setting up your phone through the Windows Live website, you have a couple of settings to enable on your Windows Phone in this settings area to improve the ability of Microsoft to find your phone. You can choose to save your location periodically for better mapping and use push notification. Microsoft cautions that the Push Notification setting will use more battery than timed notifications, so keep that in mind if battery life is a concern for you.

PHONE UPDATE

Microsoft is committed to making your Windows Phone 7 device even better than it is, so it will be releasing updates. These updates will appear when you connect with the desktop software, but you can also view and manage these updates from your Windows Phone.

If an update is available, a notification appears on your phone, assuming that you have checked the box to notify you when new updates are available. You can also choose to use your cellular data connection to check for updates, but make sure you have an unlimited data plan or are aware of the data costs before downloading files of significant size. Some updates can be performed over-the-air (OTA) and performing these over Wi-Fi might give you a better experience with faster data speeds.

ABOUT

The About page of settings is an informational page that shows you information such as the following:

+ Device Name
+ Model of Your Device
+ Software Version
+ Total Storage
+ Available Storage
+ Specific Versions of Software and Radios

One other major function found on the About page is the option to reset
your phone. If you tap the Reset button, a warning pop-up appears informing
you that you will erase all your personal content and apps, and the device will
be restored to factory settings. Tap Yes if you truly want to wipe your device
clean or No if you change your mind.

FEEDBACK

The final system setting is for feedback sent to Microsoft to improve Windows
Phone 7. There is a toggle bar to turn the feedback mechanism on or off with
one other checkbox option to use your cellular data connection to send feedback. If this is not selected, feedback will be sent via Wi-Fi or when you connect your Windows Phone to your computer.

Application Settings

Application settings are specific to the applications loaded on your Windows
Phone 7 device, and they will likely vary by carrier and manufacturer. Some
standard application settings are discussed in detail in this section, but be
aware that your particular device may have more settings available to you. The
settings covered in this section and in various other chapters include those for
games, Internet Explorer, maps, messaging, phone, camera, radio, and more
(see Figure 21-5).

You also see that some of the settings here are the same ones accessed from within specific applications discussed throughout various chapters of this book.

GAMES

The Games setting is one simple toggle bar to turn on or off your connection to Xbox LIVE. Use the available hyperlink to view the Privacy Settings Policy in Internet Explorer Mobile.

INTERNET EXPLORER

Following are available settings for Internet Explorer (described in Chapter 13):

+ Allowing cookies

+ Letting Bing suggest sites as you type

+ Viewing the mobile or desktop version of the site

+ Button to delete your history

Again, you can view an online privacy statement if you're interested.

FIGURE 21-5 Manage several settings specific to installed applications.

MAPS

Two basic functions are available in the Bing Maps settings (also discussed in detail in Chapter 12). You have a toggle to use your location and a button to delete mapping history. In Internet Explorer Mobile, you can also view the privacy statement and terms of service.

MARKETPLACE

The settings currently found under the Marketplace heading simply include a hyperlink to view and manage your Zune account settings from within the Internet Explorer web browser.

MESSAGING

The messaging settings enable you to toggle on or off text message delivery confirmations and also customize your text message (SMS) call center number. Your text message call center number should be filled out by default, so you don't need to change this in Settings. However, if you travel overseas or have a special setup with your carrier, Microsoft gives you the option to manage these settings.

OFFICE

These settings were discussed in detail in Chapter 15, and after you tap them the settings open up in a different interface than the rest of the settings, because you are now within the Office 2010 suite where these settings are managed.

Settings for Office 2010 include those for your username, SharePoint account, OneNote sync toggle, and About page, as shown in Figure 21-6.

PEOPLE

The people settings were discussed in Chapter 8 and include those for sorting and displaying your contacts and adding accounts. The account addition is similar to the System settings for Emails & Accounts. You also have control over how your Facebook friends are integrated on your Windows Phone. You can choose to just have Facebook info for your existing contacts appear or have all of your Facebook friends appear as contacts.

PHONE

Phone settings include managing your voicemail number, caller ID info, call forwarding number, and international assistance. These settings are discussed in more detail throughout Chapter 3.

FIGURE 21-6 Use the settings here to optimize your Office Mobile 2010 experience.

Your voicemail number is entered by your carrier and should not need to be changed.

PICTURES AND CAMERA

Settings for the pictures and camera functions are described in Chapter 8 and include establishing how the camera functions and what happens to pictures that you capture.

RADIO

The Radio settings consist of a drop-down list to let you select the region where you are located so that radio stations can be found for you. Most devices should have an option only for your location, so you will likely never need to access this Settings page.

SEARCH

Bing Search is discussed in detail in Chapter 11, with settings to optimize search. You can tap the toggle bar to turn on your location information to get more accurate local search results; if it is turned off, these results may not be accurate.

You can also check the box to enable Bing to suggest terms to search as you type. I find this extremely efficient and functional, so I recommend enabling it on your device.

You will also find a button to delete the search history, which deletes the previously typed search terms you entered; if you enter a lot of terms you never plan to access again, you might want to clear this out.

Related Questions

✦ How do I make a call with my Windows Phone? **PAGE 27**

✦ How do I take a photo with my Windows Phone? **PAGE 97**

CHAPTER TWENTY-TWO

HOW DO I DEAL WITH PROBLEMS ON MY WINDOWS PHONE?

In this chapter:

+ General Troubleshooting Techniques
+ What Can I Do if I Lose My Windows Phone?
+ Connection Problems

W indows Phone 7 is the most stable mobile platform ever released from Microsoft, and in extensive testing with early versions of the software, issues have been few and far between, so you should rarely experience any problems. It is a modern piece of mobile gear, though, and there are issues, real or perceived, that might occur due to specific hardware components, software glitches, other actions, or simple human error. The good news is that a majority of these issues can be solved quickly and easily by you without having to take or send the device in to the carrier or manufacturer.

General Troubleshooting Techniques

Before you visit your local carrier store or send your device back to be repaired, check through these different techniques to see if your particular issue can be fixed.

RESTART YOUR WINDOWS PHONE

The easiest thing to try first if your phone acts up is to turn it off and then on again. This solution is generally helpful for applications that may be causing issues, and by restarting your phone, you clear out the running processes and let your phone start back up.

To restart your Windows Phone, simply press and hold the Power button for a few seconds, generally about 5 seconds, and then you may see the word Goodbye appear as it shuts down. To turn it back on, press and release the Power button.

TAKE OUT THE BATTERY

Although turning your phone off and then back on again can clear out running processes and address some issues, you might need a deeper reset to clear out a problem. Windows Phone devices have removable batteries, which is helpful for those who will be out and about for long periods of time and carry spares, so you can easily slide off the back cover and take out the battery to solve an issue.

Follow your manufacturer's specific directions for your hardware, and take out the battery. Leave the battery out for about 30 seconds, and then replace the battery and back cover. Turn on your Windows Phone to see if your issue is resolved.

RECHARGE YOUR WINDOWS PHONE

It is possible that the problem you are experiencing is simply due to a battery that is completely discharged. Windows Phone 7 devices have standard microUSB ports for connecting to your PC or an A/C charger, so connect your device and let it charge. The battery indicator light and/or display on your Windows Phone should indicate charging status after you plug it in.

If you have a spare battery available, you can also try swapping it in place of the current battery to see if a low battery was the cause of the issue.

BACK TO START AND TRY AGAIN

If you run an application, and it locks up, you might want to press the Start button to go back to the Start screen and then try relaunching the application. Some applications have startup routines that check the app, and the issue may be resolved or discovered as the app is taken out of its saved state.

CHECK FOR A WINDOWS PHONE UPDATE

If you have automatic updates already selected, you should know about available updates; it is recommended that you keep your Windows Phone up to date. If you do not have this automatic check enabled, you may want to manually check for an update that might resolve the issue you are having with your device.

To manually check for an update follow these steps:

1. Tap or slide to the application launcher page.

2. Slide down the page to Settings and tap the word Settings.

3. Slide down to Phone Update and tap on it. See Figure 22-1 for the setting to check for a phone update.

FIGURE 22-1 Make sure the top box is checked so that you know if updates are available.

If there is an update available then it will be listed here on this screen. Follow the specific directions given to install the update since some are performed via a wireless connection and some via a connection to your PC.

CHECK FOR APP UPDATES

Similar to Windows Phone system updates, applications are updated from time to time with improved performance, new features, and for other reasons. If you have an application issue, go into the Marketplace hub where you can see if there are any app updates available. You can even tap the icon for the application you are having an issue with to see if that application has an available update.

RESET YOUR PHONE

If none of the techniques previously mentioned solve your issue, one of the first things a technical support customer service representative will tell you on the phone to do is to reset your phone. If you recall in Chapter 21, we mentioned how to reset your phone. To do so, simply go into the About page of your Settings and tap the Reset button. You'll get a warning to confirm your decision, as shown in Figure 22-2.

FIGURE 22-2 You get one last confirmation before you decide to wipe your Windows Phone.

What Can I Do if I Lose My Phone?

The Find My Phone settings were detailed in Chapter 21, and as discussed you can use this utility and service to find lost or stolen phones while also managing what happens to the phone if it is not recoverable. This utility will likely be used much more for those times when you simply misplace your Windows Phone, but this is a fairly common occurrence for many people.

I personally leave my phone in vibration mode most of the time because I work in an office environment, so if my phone just vibrated when I tried to find it, I would likely never find it. Thankfully, Microsoft enabled Windows Phone 7 devices in Vibration mode to still sound out with a unique sound when searched for via a web browser and the Find My Phone service.

If your phone is lost and likely unrecoverable, you should remotely wipe it as that will erase all data on your phone and return it to factory settings. This means that someone else can then set up the phone as their own, but if they try to use it with your wireless service, your carrier might be able to assist in its recovery. If not, your wireless carrier can disable service so that you are not charged for any unauthorized usage.

Connection Problems

You may experience issues connecting your Windows Phone to your PC, Wi-Fi network, cellular network, Bluetooth accessory, or other connected device, such as a pair of headphones. Most of the time there are simple solutions to solving these issues, and some may even cause you to go back and laugh at yourself for being so silly.

PC CONNECTION ISSUES

Your Windows Phone connects to your PC and works only through the Zune desktop software, so the first thing to check is that you have the latest desktop software installed. Initial connections between your PC and Windows Phone are made through a USB connection, and unfortunately PCs do suffer from USB port issues. Many USB port issues can be solved by unplugging the cable and restarting your PC before trying the connection again. Also check that there are no Windows security issues blocking Zune desktop functionality.

WI-FI CONNECTION ISSUES

Success of the 802.11 b/g/n Wi-Fi connection made from your Windows Phone 7 device is dependent on the router providing the wireless signal connected to the Internet. The first thing to check if you find your Wi-Fi having issues on your Windows Phone is the router providing the signal. Try using another device or your PC to test the Wi-Fi connection to verify it is indeed working properly.

After you have determined that the Wi-Fi access point is set up and working properly, check to make sure you actually have the Wi-Fi radio enabled on your Windows Phone. As detailed in Chapter 21, this is found in the Wi-Fi settings.

If you connect to a secured network, make sure to double-check that the password was entered correctly because this is in area in which you can easily make a mistake.

CELLULAR NETWORK CONNECTION ISSUES

Your cellular network settings should be set up properly by default. The first thing to check if your Windows Phone is not connecting through the cellular network is whether Airplane Mode is enabled. If it is not enabled and you should have a connection, jump over to the cellular Settings page to check that you have an active network and that roaming settings are properly established.

BLUETOOTH ACCESSORY ISSUES

You can use Bluetooth to connect a headset to your Windows Phone and might sometimes find that the two devices don't feel like working together. Check to make sure the devices are paired and that both have their Bluetooth radios enabled and transmitting. If you still have problems, put your headset into Pairing mode and try pairing the two together again as if you are starting over with a new accessory.

CONNECTED DEVICE ISSUES

With the ability to play Zune music and video content on your Windows Phone 7 device, you will likely use a nice set of headphones to enjoy this content. The usual issue people have with headphones is not having them plugged in all the way, so make sure your headphone plug is inserted all the way into the headphone jack.

You may also be using other accessories such as external speakers, so make sure that the devices are properly powered on and that the connections are hard and fast.

Related Questions

+ How do I launch apps? **PAGE 1**
+ Where can I learn about using Bluetooth devices? **PAGE 27**
+ Where can I find the Zune software? **PAGE 69**

+ INDEX